The Temple That Never Sleeps
Freemasons and E-Masonry Toward a New Paradigm

Josh Heller and
Gerald Reilly

The Temple That Never Sleeps
by Josh Heller and Gerald Reilly

A Cornerstone Book
Published by Cornerstone Book Publishers
Copyright © 2006 by Josh Heller and Gerald Reilly

Published by Cornerstone Book Publishers
New Orleans, LA

First Cornerstone Edition - 2006
Second Cornerstone Edition - 2014

www.cornerstonepublishers.com

ISBN:1613422369
ISBN-13:978-1-61342-236-6

MADE IN THE USA

Introduction

The time is twenty years ago. You are driving home from work when suddenly all traffic on the highway comes to a stop. Up in the distance you can make out flashing lights. A motor vehicle accident has occurred and is blocking the lanes of the highway. You realize you may be stuck in traffic for quite some time. You wish to get a message to your family at home that you are all right. While sitting in traffic, you realize that you have never written back to your parents about their new grandson. They are looking forward to receiving your letter in the mail and perhaps a couple of photographs. You promise yourself to stop at the Post Office and buy stamps one day this week. They should have the letter by next week sometime. You would phone more often, but the long distances rates are quite expensive.

Fast forward to 2005 and let us replay the previous scene. You are driving home from work when suddenly all traffic on the highway comes to a stop. Up in the distance you can make out flashing lights. A motor vehicle accident has occurred and is blocking the lanes of the highway. You realize you may be stuck in traffic for quite some time. You flip open your cell phone and call your family. You tell them that you are fine but that the traffic will delay your arrival home. Feeling somewhat better now, you suddenly realize that you have never written back to your parents about their new grandson. You reach for your cell phone once again and call your Mom and Dad. You tell them that as soon as you get home you will fire off an email and attach several digital pictures you took at the eldest sibling's recital the night before last. They should have them in about an hour.

Technological innovation has radically changed the conduct of our daily lives. We can do things faster, easier and cheaper than ever before. We have information at our fingertips and an ability to communicate with each other, around the globe, at the speed of light. Our family lives have changed; our business practices have been transformed. E-communication is now at the core of every aspect of our culture. But what about "our" Freemasonry? How has technology affected the Craft in general and ourselves as Freemasons in particular: what are the possibilities for the future?

Perhaps it is the case that computing power has doubled every eighteen months since the mid sixties and will continue to do so. Can we begin to envisage power of this sort and how it may impact on us? But, do we just sit back and allow ourselves to be swept along by its irresistible current or are we going to be a part of it and engage with informing its shape and direction. In the 1980s, with the advent of computer Bulletin Board Systems (BBS), we were able for the first time to send computer messages back forth to other computer users who were members of the same BBS. This soon evolved into BBS networks where messages were exchanged with other BBS systems that were members of the same network. This allowed for sharing messages across immense geographical distances and eventually led to the first proprietary online communities like Compuserve and Genie. Compuserve and its volunteer System Operators, for many years, hosted an online forum for Freemasons and it was the forerunner of what we have today – Internet based online communities of Freemasons from all around the world.

Having been E-masons for over seven years and 75,000 plus E-mails later, we are open to the possibility that E-masonry will grow and provide new and exciting opportunities for Freemasonry universal. But having used the term "E-masons" we must explain our understanding of it. We suggest that, "an E-mason is a Freemason for whom a part, at least, of their Masonic improvement is provided by membership of a Masonic E-group, or groups, set up for, and subscribed to, for that purpose." The "E" is an abbreviation of electronic and denotes that the activity takes place on the Internet. Based upon that, we suggest that "E-masonry" can be understood as being the total of those groups, the Freemasons thereon subscribed and the Masonic benefits that flow there from. E-Masonry may well be met with challenges, obstacles and resistance along the way although we are not aware of any degree of formal resistance or for any proscription of participation. Perhaps it should be regarded as something that is future proof and that it could aid the survival of Freemasonry's traditional values although perhaps not in a traditional format.

The use of E-communication is a cultural phenomenon, as is freemasonry itself; but have they, together, ever been considered and described in such terms? In the opening Chapter we make an initial attempt to do so as it is from such a basis that a framework can be provided. It will enable an evaluation of the emergence and impact of E-communication and E-masonry on traditional Freemasonry to be undertaken, and from which a possible mutually beneficial development could be considered.

The culture of Freemasonry is hierarchical and centralist operating through chains of command to ensure the control, conformity and the compliance of those who choose to join and remain within its ambit. Both the WWW and e-mail are upstarts and usurpers, largely outside of control or censorship of any kind. They offer levels of freedom and access beyond most peoples' comprehension. Indeed, E-masons are doing things in the relative "immunity" of a perceived "cyber-lodge" that they may not find necessary to share with the management of their respective jurisdictions. What is the likely impact of this newfound freedom? Will liberty become license and suffer decadence's customary decline and fall? Or, will declining dinosaurian freemasonry, not thriving in a changing cultural environment, adapt and survive with lemur leanness and a speed of light fitness as enabled and facilitated by E-communication? Ought the Grand Jurisdictions have reservations about their members participating in online Masonic forums? Might the member be conversing with members of "irregular" "unrecognised" or "clandestine" jurisdictions – those declared to be non-masons? Do the members mistakenly believe these online communities to by pseudo "tyled lodges"? What, exactly, can a Mason reveal to, and withhold from, Freemasons from other jurisdictions? These are but some examples of the issues posed by E-masonry today.

After World War II, a substantial expansion of Freemasonry was experienced in different parts of the globe. For various reasons this has not enjoyed sustainability and membership numbers are in significant decline. The average age of a Freemason in many lodges is likely to be in the mid-fifties, if not higher, and non-attendance is on the increase. Perhaps it is undeniable that the known and loved Masonic way of life is becoming increasing incommensurate with the demands and values of contemporary lifestyles. Could E-masonry be a new expedient that might supplement and complement traditional freemasonry and be a vehicle for change that might sustain and future-proof Masonic values?

Perhaps the most important lesson an E-mason has to learn is that his or her Freemasonry is just that – a personal view of Freemasonry. E-masons have become very surprised at not only by the differences between the two hundred or more jurisdictions around the world, but also by the dramatic differences in style, substance and form within jurisdictions. Indeed, E-masonry posses a substantial challenge to the traditional concepts of "recognition", "regular", "mainstream" and "clandestine".

This is perhaps where the E-mason's personal journey begins. He or she must soon realize that "their" Freemasonry is not the "only" Freemasonry and certainly not the only "true and correct" Freemasonry. If there is a reality in Freemasonry, and we believe there is, it must reside in the values that it espouses and this would include tolerance and respect for the personal and organizational views of the Craft, held by member Freemasons from around the world. It is a journey into the teachings of the Craft and its Working Tools. When the sum total of all the "my Freemasonry" becomes "our Freemasonry", one realizes that this not the end; it is but a beginning of days.

This initial consideration of E-masonry does not claim to be a perfect ashlar, far, far from it. But hopefully some form will have been provided for finishing in the hands of more expert workmen. However, we will have failed if it has not been shown that E-masonry, far from being a descent into ego-centricity and solipsism, is clearly, although in embryonic form, seriously human, diverse and is meeting the needs of its members by either supplementing or complementing their usual lodge activity.

The first part is an exploratory essay is a consideration of what may be understood as being seven defining cultural characteristics of Freemasonry in general and of Freemasons in particular. The characteristics are: the work ethic, the value of education, participatory citizenship, the bind of religiosity, the primacy of fraternity, the imperative of charitability and the mystery of gender. We add to that a brief examination of the impact the E-revolution may be having in some of these areas. In the second part the Moderator tells the story of the Masonic Light E-group, celebrating the length, breadth and depth of knowledge that has been disseminated and how that new understandings of Freemasonry universal are evolving. In the third part we share the remarkable responses to a questionnaire that was circulated among the Masonic Light group members. In the concluding part, with the benefit of the group's experience to date and the questionnaire responses we seek to pull together the cultural phenomena of Freemasonry and E-communication and suggest what may be ways forward that will assist to sustain the values of Freemasonry in a world very different to that into which we were born, let alone our eighteenth century forefathers.

During 2001, the Masonic Light group's second year of operation, the 9/11 tragedy occurred. There was an appeal for all the group members in the New York Metropolitan area to make contact. Experiences of those directly and indirectly involved were shared and each member was touched with the infirmities of all. Indeed and from that time, if not from before, the E-masonic word had become flesh and was dwelling among us.

Josh Heller
Gerald Reilly
2006

Table of Contents

The Temple That Never Sleeps
Freemasons and E-Masonry Toward a New Paradigm

Chapter 1

A tale of two cultures

I. The start of a journey

We have taken upon ourselves the task of considering the phenomenon of E-masonry to see how popular it may be and to find out what its practitioners are saying that it is achieving for them. This includes an initial and exploratory enquiry to see if there was any evidence that E-masonry provided anything of added value for freemasons in general or remedies for any possible limitations that may be inherent in contemporary Masonic practice in particular. The view can be taken that the practice of Freemasonry is seriously traditional and, as a benign elder statesman, it espouses a style typical of the way that things were undertaken in former times. On the other hand, E-masonry may be regarded as a precocious upstart whose legitimate place within Freemasonry is as yet uncertain and without integration.

In the home, workplace, and in the world of leisure and entertainment, E-communication has stormed in, virtually unannounced, and within a generation has dominated. It is connecting with all human activities bringing about rapid and quintessential change to all with whom, and with what, it engages. From "none per desk" to "one per desk" in twenty years is revolution not evolution. This was the length of time that Darwin had spent deliberating over the publication of his *Origin of Species.* How much survival challenge has E-communication posed, how much extinction has already occurred in its wake, and how much yet to come? The view is taken that adaptation is usually necessary to ensure survival in a changing environment. The more rapid the change, the more substantial must be the response. In light of this, it is perhaps inappropriate for Freemasonry to seek to be immune from E-communication if its essential values are to survive and thrive.

No attempt will be made to solve the philosophical mystery of the Irishman's broom, the same one that has provided excellent service for over twenty-five years albeit with five new handles and four new heads. But, the question remains, to what extent can a thing change and still be what it was? What are the values of Freemasonry that are worthy of the future and in what form are they most likely to survive? Perhaps to consider what a thing was, and is, cannot be isolated from the historical accidents of its origin. However, as environments unceasingly and relentlessly change, a thing in and of its self may have to change in order to continue to achieve, in new circumstances, a sustainable role and relevant contribution: values come in packages the values may outlive the packages. That is to say, if within Freemasonry there are values worthy of the future, there should be no resistance to their form being adapted in order to ensure their survival. The future though, is an imprecise theoretical entity. Sometimes changes have been made in organizations in order to improve future prospects but have seriously damaged the present, and failed to make a positive impact upon the future. Not all adaptations achieve survival!

Before being able to suggest a form that the future might take, it will be necessary to consider the nature of some cultural strands, that when combined, provide Freemasonry with its defining characteristics. As Freemasonry does not have a single global organization (unless the reader is a member of a conspiracy theory lodge) its worldwide manifestation must be regarded, not as monolithic, but as being very diverse. Depending on disposition, some might say that it is a "broad chapel"; others ingenuously may believe it to be "with schisms rent asunder." World Freemasonry can, perhaps, be understood as a territorially based arbitrary collection of tribes, with all that this may entail, including some exclusive policies, procedures and practices.

It would be helpful to be able to turn to a volume of Freemasonry's definitive history; however, no such publication exists. There are many books with the optimistic title, *The History of Freemasonry* but the article may not be as definite as claimed. Very broadly, the view can be taken that there have been three approaches to recording Masonic history. The first was by Freemasons themselves, and it is reasonable to suggest that much of it is romantic, highly creative and is of little appeal to contemporary audiences. These, by and large, seek to demonstrate that Freemasonry began at around the dawn of mankind itself and arrived via the Pyramids, King Solomon's Temple, and the medieval gothic cathedrals all courtesy of stonemasons organized in lodges. These histories are largely set within, and supportive of, the orthodox Judeo-Christian milieu.

Secondly, and albeit somewhat belatedly, academia has come to realize that accounts of preceding centuries may be incomplete if they do not include reference to records of Freemasonry, people who were Freemasons, and the ideas that may have under-pinned their activities. Some stunningly interesting suggestions have been made regarding the Renaissance and Enlightenment periods, the people, ideas and practices and soundly argued linkages have been suggested that may indicate connection with modern Freemasonry. These histories are largely neutral on specific religious tradition but, unfortunately, not many artisans are involved.

Thirdly, the rigour of academia, with its silence on matters that are without the benefit of orthodox standards of evidence, does not suit all. Therefore, to meet this market, there has been the spectacular rise of "New Age history." These authors propose highly creative and radical theories that emphasize an esoteric concept of Freemasonry; largely it fundamentally challenges religious orthodoxy and all that it stands for. Again, not many artisans are involved. The volume of such books currently being produced is challenging all previous levels of publications. We are aware of academia's intellectual hostility towards New Age history, and an at least equal hostility to the rewards and recognition accumulated by New Age historians and authors. This story is set to run.

This exploratory and introductory essay is definitely not a history of Freemasonry, and it is not intended to be understood as such; it is an initial consideration of over seven years' experience of E-masonry, what it may have achieved, and how it may develop. But first, what is it that makes "Freemasonry," Freemasonry and more importantly, what is it that makes a person a Freemason? As indicated above, both Freemasonry and the arrival of E-communication are cultural phenomena, and it is the confluence of their respective milieu that is being considered. We suggest that it may be helpful to avoid the consideration of any differences between "operative" or "speculative" masons. If such terms are to be considered at all, then perhaps better to consider "operative" or "speculative" lodges. We offer a definition that an "operative" lodge is a unit in the formal regulation of the construction industry of its times. This allows for the possibility that there may be members within it who are without any formal connection, whatever, to the construction industry. Whereas, a "speculative" lodge has no formal connection with the regulation of the construction industry even though, by some remote chance, there may be practicing stonemasons within its membership. It would be a routine task for economic historians to identify the lodges that might belong to either of these two categories.

We suggest that there are seven social components that, when considered in the light of Masonic traditions, combine to provide a reasonable view of the defining characteristics of Masonic culture. They are: the work ethic, the value of education, participatory citizenship, the bind of religiosity, the primacy of fraternity, the imperative of charitability, and the mystery of gender. With a most cautious retrospect, each of these aspects of culture will be very briefly outlined from earlier days to the present. The initial impact that E-communication has made in these areas will be considered and also, how this may be impacting on Freemasonry as traditionally practiced. This will provide a basis for looking at the data from the questionnaire responses, seeing if E-masonry is making a contribution, helpful or otherwise and, to suggest how E-Masonry could be developed to ensure the survival and thriving of what, of Freemasonry's values, may be worthy of the future, and in what form. Hopefully, it will seem like the same broom even though it may have new heads and new handles.

II. The Work Ethic:

For the purpose of this introductory essay, the view will be taken that modern Freemasonry has linkages with work practices on construction sites of yesteryear. (Even though this may leave us open to accusations of a romantic indulgence which may be difficult to refute.) Such sites may have contained a temporary building called a lodge in which stonemasons kept their tools and materials; slept, ate, and socialized; were received into the craft, trained and under whose roof, prices, wages and work standards were agreed. On the other hand, "lodge" may be more usefully understood as pertaining to the collectivity of the operatives. For our brief purposes, the term "lodge" will be used interchangeably. It may also have been the mechanism from which relief was provided for stonemasons and their dependents in time of need. Therefore, the stonemason's lodge may well then have been a nexus for the regulation of part of the construction industry; but as is often the case, an organization takes on a life of its own and its original purposes can become subsumed by the needs of the organization itself and other matters. A time must have arrived when there was a realization that the strength of the lodge is the mason and the strength of the mason is the lodge. This would have created an ethos in the workplace indicating that work was perhaps becoming more than just a job. Also, perhaps craftsmen of all sorts were identifying with their work. They were not just conduits of divine creativity and skills, as their own faces were appearing in paintings and sculptured scenes.

It is assumed that the main clients would have been the religious, civic and military powers. It is reasonable to believe that operative lodges would have had linkages with these powers, especially if "architects" were lodge members, and that they may well have been over and above that which was strictly necessary for the regulation of the trade. Perhaps an early perception of oiling the wheels of industry? Also, and building on that, as main clients, they each would have wished to exercise some control over the industry in order to obtain priority in times of labour and material shortages, control of prices, and control over standards. This may have led to attendance and participation within the lodge by representatives of the clients. There may have been activities and arrangements within the lodge building, conducted by lodge members that, again, were over and above what was required for the regulation of the stonemason's portion of the construction industry. Many human activities are undertaken with an embellishment of some measure of ritual; over time perhaps, this ritual takes on a life of its own and becomes, of seeming necessity, the way that things ought to be accomplished now and forever and couldn't be done in any other way – so mote it be!

Perhaps it was these additional linkages and activities that became a basis for people, other than operative stonemasons to become "members" of lodges. This trend may have increased and in combination with lodges becoming less central to, and finally no longer part of, the regulation of the construction industry; the lodges became essentially centres of social activity. Yet, and for whatever reasons, there remained a central allusion to being a stonemason, albeit of a theoretical type; or of whatever type that is denoted by the 17th/18th Century English term "speculative." But, and by whatever mechanisms, these people had become what are now known as "Freemasons" it is likely to be the case that very few of them had ever hued, cut or built with stones: but workers they were!

More through inspiration than perspiration and combining with the favourable accidents of birth, Freemasons were there numbered among the elite at the forefront of wealth creation. Monarchs and parliaments were being required to ensure an internal peace and order that would foster prosperity and facilitate the enjoyment of surplus fruits of labour. And through this and in the guise of traditional religious conformity, rational and self-enlightened mammon became righteousness (and officers of Grand Lodges).

Individual lodges began to amalgamate by uniting in constitutions, jurisdictions or obediences each being creations reflecting the historical accidents of their birth; their particular space and time. Social groupings do not operate in a vacuum; the implications of being a member of a lodge and the activities of the lodge must have been understood within the context of the contemporary political, religious, social and economic milieu. Freemasonry stood for the right of an individual to work, prosper, and be happy. Any activity by the powers that be that may have challenged this would have incurred, either overtly or subversively, a retaliatory backlash. It is variously claimed that Freemasons had significant involvement with revolutions in England, America and France. Such may well be the case, but interpretations of this are perhaps complicated by the possibility that there were Freemasons on both sides! But of course, bread can be buttered on both sides.

Freemasons may well have challenged the status quo when it has sought to interfere in the pursuance of wealth and happiness. This perhaps does seem to indicate a primacy of the work ethic and a celebration of its successful outcomes. The working tools are the means by which good work is produced; a modern speculative Freemason allegorically transfers the cutting edge of these working tools to carve out his own life of goodness. It is anticipated that in their professional lives, Freemasons will through assiduity produce outcomes of quality and integrity: these values allegorically transfer from the workplace to underpin the rest of life; that is to say, square work equals square life. Perhaps uniquely Freemasonry derives its ethic from the workplace and then applies it to the rest of life. (This perhaps explains, to some extent, the vocational basis of much primary education.) Freemasons are not expected to go bankrupt. Material success can be regarded as an anticipatable outcome of integrity and assiduity. By, in and through their good works and good lives, professionally, public and private, they believe that they are allegorically re-building King Solomon's Temple – a new world order of strength, wisdom and beauty. They are people committed to their own daily personal improvement and through their own good works they are building a better world. They are providing the means of support for themselves and their own dependents, that being the first duty of a person fit for this world and producing surpluses to be enjoyed albeit leaving some portion, without determent to self or connections, for the deserving needy. By devoting some of that surplus to the cause of the deserving needy, perhaps fitness for another world can be demonstrated. In reality, it is a system of morality that recognizes and celebrates good works which is understood as thereby building a better world for self and mutual benefit in this world and, for those who choose to believe it, in a next.

Formerly, stonemasons may have worked in gangs and any other activities were in groups organized around the demands of the workplace; speculative Freemasons have, for the last two centuries or more, met together in their lodges. However, many of these Freemasons have been employers, professionals and self-employed people with a work flexibility that enabled attendance at lodge meetings and all the other duties commensurate with the maintenance of a thriving social organism. However, perhaps modern work patterns are a challenge to the traditional pattern of lodge meetings. Also, perhaps there are increasingly more lodge members who are not from the professional and managerial work-place and do not have the flexibility to meet the demands entailed in daily Masonic "progress." Will these emerging work styles facilitate attendance at these fixed Masonic meetings and reinforce the traditional pattern of meeting? Or, is there a gulf emerging between modern work practice and the practice of Freemasonry as traditionally understood and undertaken?

In the generation since the birth of the personal computer, we have seen a dramatic change in the way these devices have, forever, changed the way many people perform the duties of their vocation. PCs and their software applications have made typewriters obsolete by allowing for a quicker means of "written" communications. We can calculate figures and process more data than ever before. We can subsequently send our electronic output to anyone, residing nearly anywhere on the globe, in a matter of seconds. The portable computer and network connection to company systems has allowed people to take more work home, or anywhere else in the world, with them than ever before. With technology driving the pace of business faster and faster, employers are enabling greater outputs from fewer operatives than ever before. This is understood as "productivity gains." While originally touted as a time-saver, use of technology has allowed each of us the time to undertake more and more work. So while the time it takes to complete a certain task may have decreased, we are now performing many more tasks at a seemingly increasing frenetic pace.

The workplace is also becoming more global. As such, there is more travel involved in many professions than ever before. This, in conjunction with the many other things that now compete for our leisure time, can make attendance at traditional meetings difficult at times. This begs the question: Does the content and substance of today's typical traditional Masonic meeting have what it takes to keep its members interested and coming back for more?

Given the spread of E-working, what might be its impact on the traditional practice of Freemasonry? What limitations might be imposed and how, if at all, might E-masonry contribute towards their mitigation. This is a fundamental consideration. But before that is examined, having claimed that Freemasonry is about the allegorical symmetry between square work and a square life, how does a person become enabled to produce square work; what does a person have to know and how is that knowledge obtained?

III. The value of education:

It has to be assumed that those who were responsible for the design and construction of large buildings were people of intelligence, education and training. It is likely that they enjoyed leading positions in the socio-economic structures of their times. Some have written on the European Enlightenment and have made mention of Freemasonry, Masonic lodges, and individual Freemasons. It would be interesting, in the case of some individual freemasons who made their mark in the mainstream world, to know how much of that could be attributed to their Freemasonry. It may well be inadequate to consider Freemasonry in its 17th and 18th Century appearances, apart from the process of Enlightenment, in its rational, romantic and radical manifestations in Europe and in the European colonial holdings. It may well be the case that the Freemasonry of those times would also have elements more recognizably as being from the earlier Renaissance. But the break with the past achieved through enlightenment was in degrees variously evolutionary as well as at times revolutionary.

An outcome of The Enlightenment was to provide earthly explanations for the phenomena that occurred on earth and the visible portion of the heavens. This was under-pinned by a growing belief that reason, rather than revelation, was the substantial basis for the acquisition of human knowledge. It not only enabled the generation of rules to indicate an order of the physical world but also rules for the management of human affairs - government. Science, the paradigm of describing the physical world in terms of prediction and control, enabled and facilitated experiments that could be repeated without any hidden human, or extra-human, attributes of the demonstrator. It may well have accelerated a rise in secularism over spiritualism, and an increasing awareness that the contribution sought to be made by religious authority into important areas of human life, may be an unfounded and unwarranted intrusion.

Perhaps it was largely in the 17th and 18th Centuries that alchemy was replaced by chemistry, astrology was replaced by astronomy and Providence was replaced by nature. Mathematics was increasingly seen as the language of the universe providing access to a means of objectively describing the hidden mysteries of nature and science. The term "civilization" has buildings connotations. It may well be the case that those who had the skills to design and supervize construction were an elite and were set apart owing to their knowledge and possession of "secrets" that enabled marking out, constructing levels, perpendiculars in square form; calculating the necessary mass of load-bearing lintels and arches. Therefore, there were those within, or associated with, the lodges who had knowledge and skills and were driven to acquire further learning.

The demands of military strategists and tacticians may well have ensured prominence for those who could deliver fortifications, undermine the fortifications of others, design artillery and build superior ships of war. It may well be the case that those who applied themselves to the emerging learning and its practical application were most likely to succeed. It would appear to be undeniable that the lodges were places that encouraged new learning above and beyond the minimum required for the regulation of the construction industry; and, that the teachers of the new sciences visited lodges and shared the newly discovered secrets of motion, mechanics, fluids and optics – some of these teachers being themselves freemasons. Therefore, those who can be identified as Freemasons were not so much skilled as artisans but rather the leading-edge designers of their era, taking a lead on technical innovation and progress and acquiring the wealth that was deemed to be the just reward for its successful exploitation.

It is reasonable to suggest that the newly emerging members of speculative lodges were indwelt with the spirit of Enlightenment, the compasses of the emblem and ritual points out the advantages of education, by which means alone we are rendered fit members of regularly organized society. Just as science could reveal cosmic order and describe nature in terms of prediction and control, so education was the basis for order and control in human affairs.

Masonic ritual exhorts the study of nature and science as a proper daily pursuit. There is also an expectation to make daily advancement in Masonic knowledge and throughout the jurisdictions there are extensive avenues for advancement and "promotions" to recognize progress. Thus, whether in the discharge of daily work of quality and integrity or in the building of a better moral world, the Freemason is enabled to do both through daily study. Therefore, it is a characteristic of Freemasonry that the apprentice progresses to become a master craftsman, a person of quality and integrity and that this is achieved through education. This surely perpetuates the Enlightenment value that humanity, as individuals and collectively can be improved through education. The question has to be asked, how much education for work, home or play is to be derived from attendance at contemporary Masonic lodge meetings?

Today, in many schools and universities around the globe, E-learning at a distance has made substantial inroads into the traditional educational processes. Accredited courses can be taken online at the students' convenience, providing flexibility for the student to perhaps maintain some employment and thereby support his or herself and/or family as well as paying for education. Perhaps following the Masonic tradition, learning is now a life-long process, or perhaps better, life itself is a learning process. Therefore continuous learning is a given for successful contemporary and emerging lifestyles.

Given the changes that E-learning has brought, and may yet bring, how might this impact on Masonic education? Are there opportunities here that E-Masonry in some form might be able to realize? Is E-learning a possible way of delivering Masonic learning through E-Masonry? It may well be, however, and before considering a possible future role for E-learning and given that the compass points out that education is the only means of fitness for a regularly organized society, what is the linkage between Freemasonry and a regularly organized society?

IV. Participatory Citizenship:

Those who have read about Freemasonry's past will be aware of claims that Freemasons were active in the English, American, and French revolutions. We are not aware of any official denial of this, and it comes to mind to ask if their involvement was an outcome related to their Freemasonry. However, an understanding of such is clouded by the likelihood that there were Freemasons on either side of each conflict. It is perhaps overly romantic to suggest that the 14th Century Wat Tyler, leader of the English Peasant's Revolt was really a Wat the Tyler of Masonic constitution. The unsuccessful insurrection concluded with Tyler's own demise by drawn sword – perhaps the only Masonic connection.

The 17th Century could certainly be described as one of revolution in England. The first half concluded with the demise of the King, and again with a drawn sword - and yet again, perhaps that is the only Masonic connection. The English historical record of this half of the Century has yet to reveal any useful detail of the existence of lodges either as buildings or as identifiable groups of people. Therefore, to suggest an organized Masonic involvement on either side is perhaps extending beyond what can be demonstrated. This was not a time of mass participatory citizenship. What little might have remained of the guild system may have been picked over by the then powers that be; although, in the dispute over sovereignty between the King and Parliament, power vacuums were perhaps being created and filled – the old order breaking down and new ways of doing things was emerging.

For most people the choice between King and Parliament was perhaps hardly informed. It wasn't as though more than a handful had a vote, and it was perhaps largely a choice of which side to die for. Whether or not a King should rule with or without Parliament, that is to say, where sovereignty should reside, is hardly a question or issue for people consumed by a daily toil against hunger, disease and poverty - the battle for survival. Unless of course they believed that one of the protagonists really held the key to a better land, either on this earth or the keys to a kingdom elsewhere. But, since the Reformation starting in the previous century, if not before, groups espousing radical forms of Christianity had been more openly questioning the status quo in general and the concept of private property in particular. Some, having sided with a victorious Parliamentary side in the English civil war, were debating with their leaders for a revised order.

If kings were those who successfully led conquests of lands and people, using the time honored means of murder, rape and pillage, then perhaps Cromwell was no different. Upon having royalty thrust upon him, his priority was the traditional kingly one of retaining his gains by making his foes, within or without, real or imaginary, the footstool of his feet. Perhaps it is the case that what was left of the guild regulation of trades, stonemasonry included, finally fell over. The Commonwealth Period may well have been a time for the reformation of social grouping, and perhaps it may be the case that it was from about this time that the term "constitution" was first applied to a document listing the aims and rules of an organization.

Other than for the House of Stuart, "Restoration" is perhaps not the most appropriate appellation for the times following 1660. The need to rebuild a fire-ravaged London and for improved military shipping, combined with a lack of serious religious conviction or leadership flowing from the King, may have provided a catalyst for scientific and technological advancement. That timber was no longer a preferred material for the re-building of London and that stone and brick were specified by regulation may have had some impact on the way tradesmen were organized in the construction industry. However, in our view, it is unlikely that speculative Freemasonry's membership was significantly drawn from among the artisans or any outside of the existing franchise.

Charismatic King notwithstanding, he was aware that he had been invited to return by Parliament, however his succeeding brother did not likewise defer and the Glorious Revolution saw his exile. Subsequent legislation can be understood as making important statements. Sovereignty resided in Parliament by virtue of a transfer of the people's sovereignty, that of the small minority who were enfranchised, to the members of Parliament. It is likely that it was from these electoral elite and the elected members of Parliament themselves that the majority of speculative Freemasons were drawn, especially from Dr. Locke's emerging Whig party. Legislation ended the principle and practice of kings ruling by Divine Right. Religious authorities also became subject to Parliament and this ended the Divine Right of God to rule through his Church, and anointed priesthood, in matters now deemed to be secular and thus the prerogative of the state. A view has to be taken on how much of this was achieved by people of Enlightenment and how many of them were members of speculative lodges. If there were any, was this activity as individuals, or, was there an ethos within the lodges that was liberal, progressive and secular that collectively supported social change in general and participatory citizenship in particular?

It may be the case that the 1723 Constitution of the self-proclaimed Grand Lodge of England, whatever that may have been, was a political document supporting a constitutional non-Roman Catholic monarchy and a tolerant established church with theological pragmatism having been cloned into the DNA of Anglicanism. Also, this Constitution may have been promoting the primacy of internal peace and prosperity with emphasis on the former to ensure the realization and enjoyment of the latter. Perhaps the age of the demonstrable and explicit sovereignty of the economy was arriving. The reason why political and religious discussion was prohibited from the lodge may not have been to prevent disputation among members at all. Rather, perhaps because there was nothing to discuss, these issues were fixed and not open for consideration. That is to say, the politics was Whig, and the religion was prosperity. The first recognised British Prime Minister, a man who personified the body politic for nearly the whole of the first half of the 18th Century, has his portrait, painted in the regalia of Grand Steward, in UGLE Headquarters, perhaps just a coincidence? The Act of Toleration was intended to supersede violent disputation on matters of theological interpretation – domestic peace and prosperity were far more important!

The spread of speculative Freemasonry through the 18th Century was substantial. In each resting place it was adapted to suit local circumstances and its development locally had a life of its own. This spread was through diplomats, political activists, entrepreneurs and the military. This included the "colonies".

In the former British colony now known as the United States of America, Freemasonry "officially" arrived in the early 18th century. The Grand Lodge of England appointed a Provincial Grand Master in 1730 for New York, New Jersey, and Pennsylvania. So begins "official" Masonic history in the Colonies. Over the next forty or so years, numerous lodges were created, warranted or otherwise, from several Grand jurisdictions, most notably under the Grand Lodges of England and Ireland. Many of these lodges existed right up until the time of the American Revolution where, no doubt, those who wished to go to war mixed with those who were loyal to the crown. It may be suggested that those who had the most to lose over "taxation without representation," were the wealthy and elite citizens of their day. It was they who perhaps saw an increasingly substantial tax burden as a threat to their pursuit of happiness and rallied their fellow citizens to their cause.

Perhaps it was in continental Europe in general and France in particular that The Enlightenment, Freemasonry, and Freemasons can be most readily identified with seriously subversive political activity. If Brother Rousseau and his Common Will, Brother Voltaire with his atheistic attacks on the ancient regime and Brother Robespierre with his cult of the Supreme Being saw a harmony between their political writing and activity, and their alleged Freemasonry, then Freemasonry may well deservedly share some of the "blame" for the Revolution: the aforementioned Brethren certainly providing the vocabulary of the revolution. This may indicate the possibility of Freemasonry, in its local and regional manifestations, being a grouping of politically active people with a common agenda. They may have been people with a shared vision of the way the world should be that was inseparable from, even synonymous with their Masonic perception of re-building the Temple of King Solomon. But this, then, does lead to considerations of Masonic secrecy and subversion.

Kings and governments are occupied with fears of enemies without and within, and are troubled by the existence, real or imagined, of secret societies. They, by definition, can only be understood as a threat. Freemasonry has been variously denounced as a secret society and proscribed, has been exempted from legislation pertaining to secret societies, and has also been openly allowed and practiced. Perhaps there is only one secret in Freemasonry and that is that there are no secrets; but, on the other hand, if Freemasonry had and still has secrets, then not having any is what Freemasons would want you to think! (Ah, the joy of conspiracy theories.)

During the 18th to the first third of the 20th Centuries, the franchise was extended in various polities. Given the position of Freemasons at the upper echelons of power there was a check and balance of influence to ensure that in the implementation of the ideals of democracy, it may well have been the case that nothing was done to significantly harm the interests of Freemasonry in general, and Freemasons in particular. Until, that was, the coming to power of National Socialism. Inherent within its ideology was a zero tolerance of Jews, a faith community who had achieved integration into all areas of society including Freemasonry. It is reasonable to believe that many non-Jewish Freemasons defied the law and provided rescue, shelter, and evacuation for "Semitic" brethren. In the UK, the arrival of a new Government in 1997 saw a requirement for Freemasons who were public sector employees, to "declare" that they were Freemasons. This was defied by some. Other Freemasons, sadly, felt forced to resign from the Craft. However, this was fought successfully by the UGLE on the basis of the European Declaration of Human Rights. (It is unlikely that many Freemasons voted for the 1997 government or had much enthusiasm for its 1998 Human Rights legislation – ironically, Freemasons were its first significant beneficiaries - who would have thought it?)

It may well be the case that Freemasonry and political activity cannot be mutually excluded. Core at the culture of Freemasonry is a strongly held view about the right of the individual, through rational and enlightened self-interest, to pursue prosperity and happiness within a liberal legal framework. If governments choose to proscribe Freemasonry or Masonic values, perhaps E-Masonry would be a seriously powerful means of resisting such a prohibition. On the other hand, E-communication may be perceived by governments as being a means for greater control. Perhaps the battle for freedom will in the future be fought in cyber-space?

Whilst the Divine Right of Kings is no more, where monarchies still exist, a successor is usually anointed by the leader of the recognized state religion. Despite the attack upon revealed religion by rationalism and materialism, many people, including Freemasons by way of ritual, and community activities, manifest the outward appearances of religious conformity. Perhaps man shall not live by reason alone.

V. The bind of religiosity:

Perhaps it is the case that it was a significant day when chimps came down from the trees and populated savannahs; stood up-right, developed enhanced dexterity, vocal range and brain processing power, and most importantly, learned to cooperate at increasingly higher levels through an increasing ability to share ideas. Some sense had to be made of dreams. The practice of burying the dead was developed and then burial of the dead with accompanying artifacts. At this point, it is reasonable to suggest that religiosity and spirituality, "the day of the Lord", had arrived. Perhaps these things can be understood as serious thoughts about relationships; that is to say, religious and spiritual needs are a seeking for satisfactory relationships on various planes and at different levels.

Perhaps the basis of religiosity lay and still lies in a seeking to make sense, coming to terms with, the apparent inevitability of physical death: perhaps it was from this perverse starting point that there was a projection back to make sense of life. Having decided on an understanding of physical death and what preparation should be undertaken in this life, systems of control and order were created to ensure conformity and compliance. This was likely to have included a respect for the sun as the highest and the life source, as well as respect for the fertility of fellow humans, animals and the land. Indeed from this there may have been created the basis for human government which can perhaps be understood as a dynamic synthesis of competition and cooperation.

It has been suggested above that kingship was the prerogative of those who had conquered people and lands. Having conquered, the kings wanted to enjoy the benefits of their spoils turning from fighters to farmers. But this conquest was only possible with the cooperation of the fighting force. How could this cooperation be obtained and maintained thereby enabling a king to enjoy his share of the spoils, his generals and other favoured their share, and also create and maintain a status quo – internal order? If the successful conquest by a king can be understood as a form of approval by a higher authority, it provides a sound and convincing basis for control, compliance, and conformity.

Initially, the emerging spaces between the influences, spiritual and secular, were not overly significant for trades-people in general and stonemasons in particular; toil is toil by any other name. It does seem that a part of the operation of guilds, each with their patron saint, would be to support and identify with church activities. Similarly there would be identification with town activities such as markets and fairs. Perhaps the most significant aspect of medieval culture was a widespread belief that there was a heaven to be gained and even more importantly, a hell to be shunned. In such circumstances, significant religious conformity can be assumed and that it is under-pinned by conviction rather than convention.

However, the 14th Century plague that wiped out, in horrific fashion, perhaps at least a third of Europe's population, may well have engendered the survivors with a concept of hell on earth. It may have led to people thinking that this life was more than just a period of proving and trial for another life. Perhaps it began to make sense, to make sense of this life for its own sake. But that is mere rationality. By the time that there may have been a significant decline in a supernaturally based meaning of life and death, religiosity was a way of life, it was the way that things were done and the important things of life were accompanied with and almost indistinct from religious form. That is to say, the outward appearances of religious conformity have greatly outlived the conviction of religious belief. Even if a religious model becomes outdated, the need to make sense of life and death remains. It is not only monks that have religious habits. It must be the case that most early speculative Freemasons conformed to, at least, some outward religious compliance. Yet, it has been suggested that there was an astonishing toleration, by presumably austere Presbyterian authorities, of the activities of 17 some Scottish lodges. This includes such strange practices as taking the mason's word, having second sight, oath-taking and irregular group worship. Even more astonishing when discussed by the church authorities, it was not considered improper for a Presbyterian clergyman to seek membership in a lodge.

Perhaps the turmoil of the 17th Century English civil war began to sow the seeds of doubt in the minds of erstwhile religious devotees. The Church was unable to trumpet a clear sound and was loosing its hold; it didn't seem to be playing a useful part in peoples lives.   Since the 18th Century, at least, the relationship between Freemasonry and religions has been volatile and less than clear. It may well be the case that some European lodges very quickly, if not from their outset, did not have a recognisable conformity with any of the major religions. For the rest, there remains the fundamental question that if a person subscribes to a religious system, it should be a complete package making sense of life and death and not needing to be supplemented or complimented by anything like Freemasonry. A religion worth its salt would not need any help from Freemasonry, but if the salt shall have lost its savour, wherewith shall it be seasoned? Freemasonry, if it is worth anything, should be capable of offering a framework to make sense of this life. It becomes very slippery when an organization that claims to be secular, and neither a religion nor a substitute for religion contains within its ritual an indication that its working tools provide a reminder and incentive to obey Divine laws that will enable access to a "Grand Lodge Above". We are at a loss to understand why some jurisdictions require a belief in the immorality of the soul and the resurrection of the body. There has to be reasons why religions are, at best, uncomfortable with Freemasonry and at worst condemn it as being "Satanic."

There has been an assumption that a person worthy of becoming a Freemason will already be religious in some way shape or form and therefore indisputably be by definition, a good man (sic). He is joining in order to make himself better and the better enabled to serve his fellow man. It is assumed that atheists, certainly "stupid" ones, are not appropriate for Masonic membership by virtue of it being true, by definition, that you cannot be an atheist and be a good person. It may be worrying that those seeking Masonic admission have to declare themselves to be good. Probably, that is the last thing that a good person would want to do and inappropriate for people on the start of a journey of improvement.

Songs that to most people appear to be indistinguishable from hymns, a necessary belief in a supreme being, in all cases of difficulty and danger putting one's trust in God and prayers are all aspects of the numerical mainstream Masonic culture. Those jurisdictions that require a belief in the immortality of the soul and the resurrection of the dead may be causing confusion given that there are some Masonic jurisdictions that will accept a professing atheist into their ranks. Some jurisdictions have affirmations taken on the Declaration of Human Rights, or other texts respected by the candidate, or even on blank pages!

It cannot be denied that some Freemasons, other than for purposes of births, marriages and deaths, have never darkened a church door. For these masons, Freemasonry is the primary source of their moral teaching and the role of Freemasonry in their lives is often indistinguishable from the role of religion in the lives of believers. Regardless of what the official position of a jurisdiction might be, through the ritual and other means, Freemasonry can and does meet some people's needs for religiosity and spirituality. It has to be understood that Freemasonry can offer spirituality that is separate from a religious basis and within the paradigm of space and time. Also, "we all like dressing-up and showing off", a quote from a world famous pioneering medical man and mason!

"Progressive" churches are using the full panoply of E-communication tools and these may be considered to be a means of residual engagement with non-attendees, a way of attracting new members, an avenue for teaching and a channel for raising funds. If E-communication can be useful for those groups that specialise in meeting needs arising from religiosity and spirituality, then why not so in Freemasonry? The revealed monotheistic religions, in their local manifestations, claim to provide belonging, fulfilment and fellowship; Freemasonry is seriously claiming to be able to offer the same.

VI. The primacy of fraternity:

Perhaps of all the cultural characteristics Freemasonry would wish to claim for itself, the quality and equality of fraternity would be primary; brotherly love being the first principle of Freemasonry. People who cooperate thereby improve their survival chances and survival was and still can be a time consuming matter. However, planning ahead and further cooperation had developed and agreed arrangements for the storage of food occurred and enabled material surpluses, over and above, levels necessary for immediate survival to be available in times of need. Perhaps during times when hunting and gathering were not possible or necessary, people came together with time on their hands and this was useful shared time: possibly this was used to reinforce cooperation by way of shared ideas through story telling and enactment: and there was also the useful discovery of narcotic substances.

Obviously, the work place became a basis for work based relationships, but within stonemasons' lodges, there may have been activities engaged with church and town that were over and above work and could be understood as social. Perhaps there is a continuum:- gregarious, cooperative and social. Perhaps life was the better for the social activities, they were enjoyable and a break from working. Perhaps social relationships and shared activities could enhance work-based relationships with regard to team building and oiling the wheels of industry.

If not before, by the 17th Century, some of the people who were joining lodges were those with the time and resources to socialise, indeed perhaps it was for socialising, in part, that they joined the lodge at all. But those who joined, at least initially, may well have had some interest in the construction industry or the operatives within it. By the 18th Century, it was the case that lodges were being joined by people who were without any apparently direct interest in the operation of the construction industry in general or in particular. What they were joining was a social club but membership was based upon serious common interests.

As professional people, politicians, civil servants, employers, clergy, retailers and self employed people, they would have been united in wishing for domestic peace and freedom in order to prosper through their own efforts and enjoy the fruits of their labours. Therefore, meetings convened in coffee houses, public houses and banqueting houses would have been occasions for keeping in touch, keeping control and having a good time too. The growth of "clubbing "perhaps indicated and reflected an increase in both economic output and social mobility and the terms "good man" and "clubbable" were perhaps synonymous. Conviviality was the right of the successful and clubbable types. There was not as yet much in the way of offices or conference centres; in London matters of business were often in the 2000 or more coffee houses, pubs and clubs.

Admission, entrance or initiation even, into some of these groups was by a ritualistic process that briefly punctuated an evening's wining and dining. In one club at least and for reasons that escape us, the admission of new members appeared to mimic the entry of apprentices into the stonemason trade. When these rituals were much later committed to print it is likely that they had extended beyond the riotous and indulgent and had assumed a life of their own. They had become as a revelation and acted as social cement binding people together just as powerfully as the dogma of a religion.   The memorising of ritual in catechistic or narrative form indicates a commitment to Masonic progress; it is on the basis of being a "ritualist" that much Masonic progression is measured and many Masonic careers are formed.

Fraternity, fellowship and brotherly love are all terms commonly found in religious language and expression. The view can be taken that they are idealistic terms to describe a bonding of people with common interests into relationships of practical cooperation. This is in the spirit of "the strength of the wolf is the pack and the strength of the pack is the wolf" or, "united we stand, divided we fall". Perhaps "fraternity, fellowship and brotherly love" overstate what is the case. For many Freemasons, their masonry substantially consists in enjoying a night out with people of similar socio-economic status, who are little if anything more than acquaintances and therefore little emotional capital is invested. Although, it can be in and through which, some genuine friendships are formed. But, it is a way of keeping in touch where matters of mutual interest could be considered, strategies created and action plans designed and delivered.

Great prosperity has been generated through economic individualism and whilst there is the need for cooperation, perhaps this is perhaps undertaken with minimum emotional capital. Perhaps fraternity, fellowship and brotherly love can be understood as, "use and be used". That is to say, the Masonic culture is dominated by the work ethic, production and output. As Freemasons, we are what we do. The culture demands that we are useful; we are measured by our achievements. And, nothing seemingly wrong about that comes to mind. A Freemason, after he or she has been initiated into light, is on a life-long journey; and, after safely crossing the River Jordan, allegorically builds with King Solomon, a temple of goodness and plenty: this can be understood to create and maintain a world of internal peace and prosperity and the freedom to enjoy it.

Fraternity, fellowship and brotherly love may appear to presuppose shared physical space. But, that may not necessarily be the case. A verse in the Christian New Testament refers to the possibility of whom having not seen ye love. Maybe significant human relationships could be created via E-communication, perhaps reinforced and maintained by occasional meetings but much less than that previously considered as being necessary in traditional freemasonry. It may be the case that current patterns of socialising fall into three chronological groupings: the first being that of the pre WWII generation, this was male dominant and featuring large was a limited social experience for the female whose attention centred on the domestic and maternal role.

The post WWII baby boomers entered adult life with the wage of the female far more significant and a tendency to socialise around the needs and activities of children. Current young adults in relationships tend to socialise together and where there are children, the domestic role of the female cannot be assumed.

The traditional demands and means of progressing in Freemason may not be compatible with the emerging social milieu. Fraternity may be enjoyed in ways other than spending hours at a festive board, learning and practising ritual and attending to the business affairs of lodge or province. Perhaps it is the case that the values of Freemasonry can be preserved and sustained through less social contact or through a contact that involves partners and off-spring. Perhaps fraternity could become something local and inclusive. Perhaps it is possible to socialise in E-space.

VII. The imperative of charitability:

Tradition has it that tradesmen's guilds provided material support in times of genuine need, accident or emergency for colleagues and their dependents. Someone who is a practical friend in times of need is a friend indeed. Workplace based social groupings occurred in taverns and other meeting places where members would place contribution into a box for re-distribution in times of need. Some of this ethos can be seen in the credit union activity over the last century.

However, having acquired wealth and the risk of needing charity receded, a more pressing issue was to be able to enjoy the fruits of wealth without let or hindrance. It has therefore been necessary for the wealthy to devote some of the riches into protection; that is to say, to pay for walls and moats around their homes, private armies, private security guards and state policemen. It is the case that those with nothing, have got nothing to lose. Therefore there is a price to be paid by the wealthy to keep the poor passive – to prevent then from either staving or revolting. In modern times this is largely achieved through taxation - a state run protection racket?

Different religions at different times have different views on almsgiving. Some have linked poverty and bankruptcy with sin, others have questioned the concept of private property and therefore a clear picture does not emerge. But, there is this pervasive concept of the re-distribution of wealth whether by the state through taxation, through private giving to institutional charities or by handing out change to a beggar in the street. After paying their dues in the most tax efficient manner, Freemasons choose the basis for a further distribution of some of their own wealth. Many Masonic jurisdictions have created their own charitable funds or have "adopted" other well-known charities for whom to raise money. It is certainly true, that charitable giving has become most seriously embedded in today's mainstream Masonic culture.

In as much as it wishes to be "seen" at all, some jurisdictions wish for Freemasons to be seen as being charitable. But, perhaps some tensions do arise. Some Masonic constitutions urge their membership to give charitably without detriment to self or connections. Yet, the holy volume upon which some take their obligations says, when giving let not your left hand know what your right hand is doing. Similarly, this same volume urges that alms be given in secret. But, as charitable giving may be being used to lever respectability, some Masonic organizations may be insisting on publicity for their giving. For some recipients that may be problematic; although they are happy to be the beneficiaries of Masonic charity, do not wish to be seen in so doing. The implication is that in taking Masonic beneficence, there is a tacit, at least, identification with Freemasonry and its values. The writers are aware of organizations that are openly hostile to Freemasonry yet accept from its charity, albeit in secret. This poses a challenge to such organizations and to Freemasons; do we wish to impose recognition as a condition for charitable giving?

Given the work ethic, material surpluses and re-distribution of wealth, it may be the case that Masonic good works are almost exclusively demonstrated in charitable giving. However, the view could be taken that as a vehicle for charitable giving, Freemasonry is a most inefficient model. The costs of premises, insurances, taxes, staff, regalia, festive boards and more are substantial and probably exceed what is given to charitable causes. Therefore the view could be taken that Freemasonry must seek justifications of its existence by achievements other than broken columns and relief chests; surely it cannot justify its existence and traditional modus operandi solely on the basis of being a charitable organization.

It is the case however that much charity that is given, is through community activities and forms of fund-raising that would appear to be labour and time intensive. But without these, perhaps the funds would not be raised at all; and perhaps some social bonding is achieved between masons and their families and between freemasons and the communities they seek to serve. Surely, if busy people want to give, e-communication, tax efficient mandates and the like, must appear attractive. But, again, without the social pressure, perhaps people might not do it. Is not the success of the ubiquitous raffle proof that people will only give in the hope of obtaining a reward?

Is there any altruism? If people are giving only to gain reward in the next world, how can that be good? If people are only giving to obtain gain in this world, again, where is the virtue? Perhaps being able to give proves that a person has been financially successful. E-Masonry provides a medium for giving to be on a sound, silent and efficient basis. Is that a way forward and will it raise enough? Might on-line giving be enabled to enjoy Masonic recognition?

VIII. The mystery of gender:

The view was taken that it was not good for man to dwell alone, woman was therefore created and the rest is history, but perhaps increasingly becoming "herstory". Until modern times the world of work and wealth creation was male dominated. The two 20th Century World Wars were substantial catalysts for change. Human Rights Declarations and local legislation, in some parts of the world, are being used to equalise the opportunities and rewards of the workplace. Increasingly, work-place tasks are being designed to ensure that they can be physically undertaken by a workforce of either gender. In some parts of the world what remains of a "glass ceiling" may largely be indicating a female preference for a child-care role rather than career continuity; although, why shouldn't both be possible and be supported? It may well be the case that some societies are increasingly developing child-care arrangements to attract and encourage both parents to work and pursue careers. Two producers are two consumers that may be of interest to the global corporations. Perhaps somewhere in this world there are female stonemasons; presumably, they would not be denied membership of an operative lodge.

The lead and participation in the world of education is increasingly becoming gender neutral. Some results are indicating that females are in an intellectual lead.

Where monarchy remains, it would appear in most that the first-born is the heir regardless of gender. Whilst female universal suffrage is fairly recent, there have been female lead politicians. That there are not more females in politics is again perhaps because of choosing a child-caring role, but that may be changing.

Within the leading religions of the world there remains the view that there are different roles for males and females and this precludes a significant leadership or teaching role for females. Freemasonry is largely a male only organization being in many of its manifestations a celebration of "The fatherhood of God and the brotherhood of man"; the male loading of these terms is perhaps convenient, emphasising and supporting male dominance and exclusivity: it also under-pins a cultural link between Freemasonry and the major religions. There does exist levels of challenge from within the major religions that are desirous of enhancing the role of females to that of equal status, but perhaps that is not as significant as the challenge from secularism. Given the essential proselytising nature of religions and the imperative for expansion there may be pressures to view gender on more equal terms. For an organization to thrive it must be relevant. If the spirit of the age is increasingly gender neutral any organization that cannot adapt to this environment may fail to survive. Perhaps an even firmer view can be expressed, if an organization is worthy of the future it will absorb the realities of social time and space.

Socialising, that is to say utilising time and money that is surplus to the needs of survival, may be an aspect of life over which freedom of choice can be exercised. But because of the traditional female domestic and child-care role, males largely socialised with males and only on special occasions were alternative arrangements made for "the ladies". Perhaps this led to social time being masculine and males behaving in ways that they would not, if they in the company of females; males possibly wish it that way but that preference may be on the decline. Also, because Freemasonry was and is largely male only, spouses may have taken some comfort from knowing that the challenge to the relationship was confined to the time spent, the money spent and the alcohol consumed. It did not, and largely does not, involve a real or imagined risk of rival females, although some, aristocratic no less, wives did check to ensure the exclusive masculinity of the meetings. It may well be the case that there would be significant spouse pressure on males attending mixed Masonic meetings, yet may it be remembered that the average age of a Freemason is nearly sixty. Again, the workplace is increasingly becoming gender neutral.

Given the shared roles of male and female in contemporary partnerships, any charitable giving is a joint contribution, something that it is likely to be a mutual contribution in participation as well as in the amount given. A dollar in the broken column is 50c from the wife.

Females in Freemasonry may have begun as an 18th Century Continental European phenomenon. Currently there are jurisdictions open to females only and mixed-masonry known as co-masonry. The former enjoys a measure of toleration as it doesn't affect what the males do and is not a risk to relationships; the latter perhaps incurs a significant measure of unease.

E-Masonry may not have such problems as interaction is held in cyberspace. Of course, E-masonry has led to members travelling and meeting with one another but it can hardly be called a dating agency; indeed freemasonry, with all that it entails, would be a very inefficient way of boy meeting girl – the antithesis of speed-dating. However in business, politics, religion and life in general, the role of the female is changing and it may not be clear what forms nuclear families of the future may take. Perhaps the view can be taken that the needs of economies, both macro and micro, will drive all agendas in general and that of gender roles in particular.

IX. The journey thus far

This opening essay has been an attempt to provide a general overview of seven aspects of culture, how they have been influenced by Freemasonry and, when taken together, provide an indication of the distinctive culture of Freemasonry and Freemasons as it may have been and how it may appear today. We have touched on the cultural phenomenon of E-communication and how it may be impacting on Freemasonry in general and Freemasons in particular.

Freemasonry is distinctive in that when it comes to how a life should be lead, the model is the workplace and work. The Freemason seeks to become an expert worker through assiduity, a commitment to excellence and a life-long learning process. At different stages, new working tools are provided and their use in the workplace is explained. Then, the allegory is developed and lessons from the technical use of these tools are applied to the rest of life. A Freemason is expected to be a successful workman being able to provide for his own dependents with surpluses for the pursuit of personal happiness and some left over for the deserving needy; all these possible because of the way he works.

A Freemason becomes skilled through a learning process and, with the authentic ring of modernity, is expected to continue in lifelong learning with respect for people who are of learning. Education is the one means alone by which we are rendered fit members of regularly organised society.

But let us be clear about this society. Within the structures of Freemasonry there are members of the elite; entrepreneurs, the good and the great, the movers and shakers. They are there at the pinnacle of influence; they are members of governments, senior civil servants, captains of industry and members of royal societies. Perhaps they are not composing as high a percentage of the Masonic membership as in former times but from a dilution of numbers can not be inferred a dilution of influence. The politics of Freemasonry is the celebration of the individual to pursue wealth and happiness and for this to be enabled and facilitated by an appropriate level of state intervention; this is known as liberal democracy. Whether this is achieved by Freemasonry in general or by individual Freemasons in particular is a very complex question but it ensures that there is no need for freemasons to engage in political disputation. The political imperative is beyond doubt; just enough government, and no more, to ensure internal order, economic growth and the opportunity to enjoy it. However, it would appear that the best of political systems need a metaphysical under-pinning. Given mans disposition to religiosity, there is no better means for control, compliance and conformity than when support for the political and economic status quo is inextricably linked to a faith system.

There were times when most explanations of events natural and human included the intervention of agencies that were outside of the paradigm of space and time. Peculiar systems of morality were formed to make sense of this life, the promise of eternal security for the faithful and obedient; eternal flames for the non-compliant and all of this to be delivered in something beyond space and time. Yet, even though these eternal promises and threats had begun to loose their potency, outward religious conformity continued and continues.

Masonic ritual is largely based upon religious texts and Freemasonry is believed by many to be something to accompany ones stated religion. Some believe that Freemasonry is only for monotheists yet others believe that there is a pantheist tradition within Freemasonry. Most religious authorities condemn Freemasonry. Atheist-tolerant freemasonry may be small but exists. Freemasonry defines itself as being a peculiar system of morality, veiled in allegory and illustrated with symbols. Could that not be a superb definition of any religion? A very confused picture of Freemasonry and religion emerges, with demarcations if any, being without any clear indication of where one ends and the other may begin. Religious habits die hard. Religions have their members bonding in a shared understanding of existence and eschatology. The Fatherhood of God and the Brotherhood of Man seem like religious concepts and perhaps that is where they should remain. What can be a basis for a distinct and separate binding of Masonic lives?

Perhaps learning the ritual and progressing through the floor-work provides an espirit de corps, the lodges of instruction being the incubators of fraternal relationships. Equally, and as is in all forms of life, planning events and activities brings people together in various degrees of bonding and some friendships are formed. But, what of relationships that are formed within families, nuclear and extended, school, college, the workplace and the neighbourhood, are these not more binding than the occasional meetings at a lodge? Of the number of masons any one mason knows, how many would he call a friend? Acquaintances they are with similar outlooks on life in terms of cooperating with each other to support the practical values of freedom, order, wealth creation and the pursuit of happiness. We can all eat, drink and be merry with that.

Yes, in most Masonic jurisdictions there is the chest from which relief can be made available for a brother in need and/or for his dependents although this can be little more than token compared with state sponsored welfare provision. The convivial ambiance inducing a sense of well being can be an effective means for raising awareness of the needs of others outside of Freemasonry, but perhaps the growth of this type of charitable giving is a more recent Masonic innovation.

But, it does seem to dominate. The impression could be given that the raison d'etre of Freemasonry is to be charitable and is now being seen as thus to be the case. But given the complexity of the Masonic modus operandi it must be about more than charitable giving. Do Freemasons obtain self-respect by giving to charity; is it cathartic or some form of conscience money? Is it buying a way to heaven? Is giving through masonry their only charitable giving? Why does the leadership of Freemasonry make so much of it other than to buy respectability and justify the Masonic status quo? Is it not the case that the freedom to create wealth is informed by some social justice and that people with material surplus should re-distribute some wealth in ways that will promote the well being of those who enjoy less of the of the advantages of nature and nurture. Anything that can usefully span the gulf between rich and poor, bringing the two nearer rather than further apart, is the needy occupation of good people, both male and female!

The gender question is vexed. It is about whether or not the role of a female is different to that of a man. If people in relationships have some separate leisure pursuits, it may provide useful space in the relationship. But Freemasonry is not a hobby; it is a way of life. It is too important to be confined to the male of the species and is unsustainable given that the workplace is becoming increasingly gender-neutral. Also, females are excelling in all areas of further and advanced education. It is in the religions that this difference of role remains and that takes us back to the unsatisfactory confluence of Freemasonry and religion.

Perhaps it is the case that e-groups, especially the Masonic Light group, or ML for short, with its celebration of diversity, have demonstrated that female Freemasonry is an undeniable and delightful reality and that to make a distinction between female only and co-masonry is trivial and unconvincing. There is nothing in the practice of Freemasonry that cannot equally be achieved by a female.

And so we have it. Freemasonry has arrived at the dawn of the 21st Century. However, the view can be taken that it is in the clothing and the mindset of a much previous generation. We believe that Masonic values are a cultural phenomenon that is worthy of the future. We are considering the possibility that E-masonry might be able to contribute to a modernisation and future proofing of Freemasonry as traditionally practiced. But before a view can be taken on what form this might take, we must undertake an examination of the seven-year experience of a significant e-group and decide what may have been achieved, or otherwise, to date. Following that, we must examine what ML members have said about their experiences with E-masonry and see if there are indications of a future-proofing confluence. Then, we will conclude by combining our view of the Masonic culture with what our members have said and suggest possible ways forward.

Chapter 2
The Masonic Light Group Story

Since 1993 I have been fortunate to have from the 5th Floor, a panorama overlooking the small town in which my employment is found. When partaking of this view, I was always greeted by the double-headed eagle logo adorning the side of the local Ancient and Accepted Scottish Rite Cathedral, located just a few blocks away. Also on this site was the local Masonic Center with its square and compasses prominently displayed in the front of the building. I surmised that the two buildings served two related fraternal groups, but I did not know just who these Freemasons were or what was their purpose might be. I grew more curious and devoted an increasing amount of time reading internet newsgroups about Freemasonry as well as a few books on the subject that were available from local bookstores. From my introductory investigation I was unable to discern if Freemasonry was either descended from medieval stonemasons or from the legendary Knights Templar. What I did take away from my reading, correct or otherwise, was that Freemasons of yesterday and today are not only men of honour who cherish the time honoured traditions and practices of those who came before them, but men with vision, energy and courage to champion the ideals of liberty, learning and fraternity. This sounded like an organization that I might like to join!

During one of my research sessions on the Internet, I decided to contact the Grand Lodge of Pennsylvania and ask about membership as I did not know anyone who was a member of any Masonic lodges in my area. It was not long until I was congratulated for "asking" and presented with a generic petition to join a local Masonic lodge. In a short time, I made the acquaintance of several local Freemasons and we hit it off. I submitted my petition which was co-signed by my new Masonic friends and was balloted on, accepted, entered, passed and raised in 1999.

Prior to becoming a Freemason, many of the internet based discussions I was able to witness were in public Usenet newsgroups. On the alt.freemasonry newsgroup I found many Freemasons congratulating each other on each new degree received as well as answering general questions about the Craft from people like me who, at the time, were not members, but may choose to join in the future. Much of the rest of what I witnessed had to do with "anti-masons". I had never heard of an anti-mason and was largely unaware of the various religious fundamentalists and conspiracy theory fanatics who are convinced the Freemasonry is something from which an individual needed to be "saved." Imagine that! Freemasonry was considered a cult or some sort of global subversive group intent on taking over the world and creating a "New World Order"!

I read the articles, papers and books published by various conservative and extremist "anti-masons". From devil worship to global conspiracies, it all seemed non-sensical to me. If this was a dangerous and powerful group, why are their local meeting halls and auditoriums clearly marked and sometimes used by various other community organizations? Why were so many revered figures in history known Freemasons?

I concluded that those groups and individuals espousing anti-Masonic rhetoric were clearly unconvincing. In my researches nothing whatsoever was found that supported such claims. I therefore decided to go forward and figure out just how to become a Freemason.

I was not sure quite what to expect in and of the lodge and of its members. In my reading on Freemasonry, there seemed to be so much to learn about the teachings, symbolism and philosophy of the Craft let alone the history of a fraternity that is some hundreds of years old. I looked forward to what the lodge and Freemasonry could teach me.

I received the three degrees of Craft Freemasonry, had my dues card, my proficiency card and was now ready and looking for more light. Alas, I found that there was nothing more my lodge could offer in terms of structured Masonic education other than our School of Instruction, but its purpose is largely to teach the local lodge officers the rituals used in the Craft workings. Yes, The Grand Lodge of Pennsylvania organized a few events per year, but what about my lodge? I wondered why there were no structured educational programs for the newly raised Master Mason at the local lodge level. I realized then that not only is Freemasonry a path of personal exploration, but one that is usually undertaken alone and without too much guidance from those who have commenced earlier along the Masonic pathway. Sadly, I was finding that many of those who were traveling before me were not on a journey that was being facilitated by structured education.

While searching for more light in Freemasonry in the spring of 2000, it became clear to me that there was a need for an email discussion group on which all the facets of Freemasonry could be considered. I had been involved in one particular email group, The Rosslyn Chapel E-group, which had a tangential interest in Freemasonry; however it was not the appropriate forum to discuss the Craft and solely the Craft. Finding my own Masonic education to be lacking and certainly slow-going in the lodge, I created the All Things Masonic Email group for just that purpose – learning about all things relating to Freemasonry. I had no idea how I would run this group. I wondered how I would be received as a Discussion Moderator of such a vast topic as Freemasonry without having much of a Masonic background. Would anyone sign up? Would anyone learn anything? What is the difference between a leap of faith and a leap in the dark?

A number of Freemasons from the other online communities of which I was a part joined the new group and quite rapidly we grew to over 50 members. From the outset members emailed and exchanged views on many different Masonic topics and the exchange of knowledge was both pleasurable and profitable and seemed to be meeting a need. There seemed to be no limit in sight to the range of questions that were being asked, especially as there were so many questions with, seemingly, no one "correct" answer. I also quickly discovered that there is much about the origins of Freemasonry that is not available from primary historical sources and which is without the benefit of a learned consensus. How surprised I was! As the months passed, we steadily increased our membership levels with Freemasons joining from each of the continents. Many found the ability to hold informal discussions about our lodges and Freemasonry in general, with a diverse and interested fellow group of member Masons, to be an injection of fresh air into their own Masonic journey. However, little did I know that the group's entry into diversity had just begun.

As we approached the end of the group's first year of existence, we had a new name, the Masonic Light group, or ML for short, a new website at http://www.masoniclight.org and the group had over 125 members, with a delightful assortment of regular contributors to the list. Then, out of nowhere, came a surprising membership application into my email inbox. The application for membership into the Masonic Light group was sent by someone claiming to be a woman! Was this some sort of mistake? Perhaps this was joke? The ritual with which I was now somewhat familiar clearly indicated that no woman could be made a Mason.

I had been raised to the Sublime Degree of a Master Mason for just over a year and had yet to travel and visit lodges outside of my jurisdiction, but clearly, I thought, this was not something I expected to find considering the Ancient Landmarks of the Craft and oath and obligation I had taken at the altar. It did not take much searching through the Internet to discover that there were indeed Masonic organizations throughout the world that admitted not only men, but both men and women on equal terms and yet others that admitted just women. What an eye-opener! But what did this mean?

I began to research terms like "regular", "recognized" and "clandestine" in a Masonic context. The American practice of some type of territorial exclusivity was also something that was new to me and of necessity became a significant part of my research. I started to understand that the Freemasonry that I knew and loved was not the only Freemasonry in the world. This, in turn, lead to learning about Prince Hall Freemasonry and the various socio-political workings of how various Masonic jurisdictions around the world maintained, or did not maintain, relationships with one another. My head was spinning! Surely, I thought, the Working Tools about which I had been instructed could not discriminate in the hands of any sincere workman regardless of race, color, creed or gender. Should such a tangled web of inter-relationships exist for any "good" reason? As I began to ponder that question, I remembered I had a more pressing decision to make. Was I or was I not going to recognize that this lady Freemason was as regular as required and admit her to equal membership of the Masonic Light Group?

Yes. I made up my mind at that moment that the Masonic Light group was going to permit ALL Freemasons into the group. Who was I, I thought, to be judging if another person's flavor of Freemasonry was not "good enough" to be included in the discussion list? After all, the Masonic Light group is not a tyled lodge meeting. We do not use nor discuss any modes of recognition or passwords of any degrees. What harm could come from allowing this lady Freemason into the group? I was willing to stand on those principles and if a mass exodus of existing Masonic Light members began, then so mote it be. There was no uprising from anyone when I admitted the first Prince Hall Freemason despite the lack of recognition of Prince Hall Freemasonry from numerous "mainstream" Masonic jurisdictions. I had not even given that decision a second thought as the Grand Lodge of Pennsylvania does recognize the Most Worshipful Prince Hall Grand Lodge of Pennsylvania. How did this particular recognition interact with the practice of "territorial exclusivity"? I wondered whether it might just be selectively applied to meet the needs of a particular organization at a given time. But what did I know? I thought, however, that by accepting a lady Freemason into the Masonic Light group I just might be pushing things a bit too far as far as the member were concerned.

After consultations with some of the founding members of the group, I admitted the lady Freemason into the list in late March of 2001 and waited by the computer for the reaction of the membership to arrive via Email. I expected that there may have been a loss of between 25 and 50% of the group membership because of this decision. I wondered how many other Freemasons, especially the members of the Masonic Light group were aware of Co-Masonry and other "un-recognized" Grand Jurisdictions. I mentally stood firm as I believed (and still do) that this was right; all I could do was wait, watch and get ready to defend my decision.

The reaction from the group was one I could not have predicted. While I certainly engaged in numerous private email discussions during the next several days, the net result was that our newest member was warmly welcomed into the group. Net membership loss was astonishingly just 3! While I was pleasantly surprised and delighted at this outcome, it was not until many months later that I began to see the forest for the trees.

Over time, the Masonic Light group has welcomed numerous lady Freemasons into membership. We have also welcomed Freemasons from many Masonic jurisdictions that are not considered "Mainstream". "Mainstream" is a term some E-Masons have used to describe the regular, recognized Masonic jurisdictions that most people are familiar with; the "Freemasonry" of George Washington, Benjamin Franklin and Theodore Roosevelt, for example. Masonic Light has welcomed members from Le Droit Humain, American Federation of Human Rights, Ancient and Primitive Rite of Memphis-Misraim, The Grand Orients of Italy, Austria and France and many other "unrecognized" jurisdictions right along side of their "recognized" counterparts, for example, the United Grand Lodge of England, The Grand Lodge of Pennsylvania and many more. There are Masonic Light members from more than 150 different jurisdictions. As far as the Masonic Light group is concerned, what matters most is the individual. Masonic Light does not involve itself in the various machinations of the Masonic jurisdictions. Further, perceptions of regularity and recognition are considered in later Chapters and there is an indication that there may be something less than rigor underpinning the positions that some jurisdictions are taking.

That being said, the authors are aware that some unscrupulous people have created pseudo-Masonic organizations to sell Masonic degrees to unsuspecting men and women who may interested in joining Freemasonry. These "bogus" organizations are the subject of study by several reputable Masonic researchers. While the Masonic Light group does not discriminate based on a Freemason's Masonic jurisdiction, the group does encourage all of its members to keep an eye out for the degree "hucksters" who allegedly are only interested in making money from unsuspecting persons.

So what does this say about the Masonic Light group? It says that we have diversity on all fronts. We have different rituals, different dress codes, different educational process etc. What we all have in common is the desire to improve ourselves in Freemasonry; to improve ourselves in order to make the world a better place for everyone to live in. We accept Freemasons in the richness of their diversity; the only thing we will not tolerate is intolerance itself.

Diversity in Freemasonry is perhaps not seen in as positive a light as diversity in the workplace, schools, and neighborhoods. Mainstream Freemasonry does not accept women members. That would violate the Ancient Landmarks of the Freemasonry although there is not in existence a set of "Landmarks" upon which every mainstream Grand Lodge agrees. But that is the subject for a subsequent publication! Mainstream Freemasonry only requires that a candidate professes a belief in a supreme being, yet many jurisdictions include theological affirmations such as immortality of the soul or the belief in the resurrection in the body. Certainly these affirmations would exclude men who are members of various faiths.

Unfortunately, racism would seem to have played a part in the Masonic record as indicated by the history of the separate "Prince Hall" Grand Lodges throughout the United States. Even today, some of the Prince Hall Grand Lodges are not recognized by their Mainstream counterpart Grand Lodges. In fact, in some areas, it is not at all uncommon for an African-American who is interested in Freemasonry to be "directed" to the Prince Hall Grand Lodge within the jurisdiction so as the potential candidate might be more "comfortable". The question arises, whose comfort is really being considered? Diversity is one part of mainstream Freemasonry that I believe needs to be improved upon if its values are to survive.

Since the inception of the Masonic Light group, we have had nearly 2,000 different Freemasons from more than 160 different Masonic Jurisdictions taking part in the group's activities. More than 75,000 email messages have been exchanged between members. The amount of information shared about how Freemasonry is practiced in various lodges, jurisdictions and geographical areas around the world, in all their glorious similarities and differences, has been incredibly revealing. What communication medium could possibly compare or compete with this. Most significantly of all, personal relationships have been formed between individuals of very differing Masonic perspectives and backgrounds, which otherwise would not have been made and people who have become good friends would have otherwise never met.

Indeed, some of the greatest joy I have derived from being an E-Mason has been experiencing all of the highs and lows of getting to know many of the individual Freemasons who have joined the Masonic Light group. As in most social settings, certain people tend to "hit it off" and a rapport develops between them. It is fascinating that this occurs without either party having ever met, spoken or having seen a picture of the other person. I have witnessed many friendships develop and some have developed into strong and what I would daresay might prove to be, lifelong Masonic partnerships. From Israel to Greece, the Netherlands to the USA, the USA to Hong Kong, Ireland to Turkey, Masonic Light group members have traveled great distances to put a face to words they have read on the computer screens many times before. As Moderator of the group, I have received numerous Emails of "thanks" and pictures of Masonic Light group members getting together and meeting for this first time. Bringing people together in this way is truly a great pleasure. Notice there is no mention of Masonic jurisdiction, race, color, creed or gender in this context. Such things are not relevant. Yes, if the two individual's jurisdictions happen to share recognition then the two of them could attend a tyled Masonic function, but it is not a priority. What has been priority is sitting down, breaking bread and getting to know the person that you had had only previously known electronically. Isn't it amazing that Freemasonry has the power to bring people together like this? Perhaps the bonding and lasting friendships that are developed like this, is one of the "real" secrets of Freemasonry.

To give but one example, we need only to look to the tragic events of September 11, 2001. Your authors were quite moved by their feelings for the Masonic Light members who may have been in the New York City area. Many group members from around the world were anxious to hear that their fellow Masonic brothers or sisters were safely out of harms way. We were all so relieved when all of our area members sent messages to the group to say that they were safe. It was this specific event that drove home to your authors that these electronic relationships were real and quite strong. We were surprised to feel just as strongly about our E-Mason friends as were about those friends with whom we come into physical contact with on a regular basis! To say we learned a great deal about ourselves that day is not an understatement.

The Masonic Light Group has experienced its share of pain. Several active members have passed away over the years, leaving us with many wonderful memories, and some regrets about never having been able to meet them face-to-face. We are aware of certain group members who have battled serious illness, fires and other natural disasters. Perhaps none of these is quite as painful as that felt by the members who have buried a child or grandchild. The group provided an outlet for expression for some and a retreat to some semblance of normalcy for others. The sharing by group members of their personal experiences, both personal and Masonic, has been quite an education for us.

Moderating the Masonic Light group for more than six years now has been an investment and return in Masonic education I could not have received from anywhere else. Not only are there dividends in Masonic education, but also in learning to deal with human diversity. When beginning to interact with people from many different socio-cultural-economic backgrounds, it is important that one's written communications are clear and concise. There are numerous issues of vernacular, idioms and humor that are difficult enough to completely understand when speaking face to face let alone via electronic communication. E-mail communication in which you can not see another person's face, hear the inflection in their voice or witness their body language can sometimes be difficult to fully assess. Often words can be easily misconstrued, misunderstood or even be unintelligible. As the Masonic Light group grew in membership from wider geographical areas with persons whose primary language is not English, it became apparent to most members that the language of our email dialogues must be written with just that in mind. By that I mean that one needs to concentrate on writing in a clear and concise format without slang or other words and phrases that may look "Greek" to a reader whose first language is not English.

The group has undertaken many special events in order for its members to have fun, improve their communication skills and learn more about Freemasonry in the process. The Masonic Light group has held several online chat-sessions with several notable Masonic authors including, Michael Baigent, Robert Lomas and Tim Wallace-Murphy, some of whom we count among our lurkers. The group has also conducted a Masonic essay contest, a Masonic logo design contest as well as having a "back-to-school" program where several Masonic booksellers, also Masonic Light group members, worked in conjunction with the Masonic Light group to provide a Back-To-School discount on all Masonic books. We have also had Henley and polo shirts made and sold with our winning group logo neatly embroidered on the front; giving a portion of the proceeds to our "adopted" charity of the year. Each year, the Moderator "adopts" a different International charity and asks that any group members who are so moved and any that ask about donating money to the Masonic Light group kindly consider donating to the groups adopted charity. In addition to all of the ad-hoc topics which come up inside the group, several of the Masonic Light members have volunteered to author recurring postings on a topic of their choice. For example, we have one brother who authors a regular posting entitled "From the Fellowcrafts' Corner", another entitled "Mackey and more" and yet another called "Rhyme and Reason" which is a look at some Masonic poetry. There is something for everyone on the Masonic Light group.

I have always believed that the membership of the Masonic Light group consisted of member Freemasons who have an above average interest in the teachings of the Craft and Freemasonry in general. A Freemason with less interest would certainly not spend their free time in search of online discussion on the subject. Surprisingly, I found that I was not alone in being wholly unaware of the existence of Co-Masonry and other orders which are considered clandestine or unrecognized before my E-Masonry experience taught me to question the meaningfulness of such appellations. I have received various Email correspondences over the years from members who were just as surprised as I was when they found out that there are lady Freemasons and some that live not too far from their own neighborhoods. They further went on to say how much they enjoyed learning about Masonic diversity whether or not they took part in the active conversations within the group. These are interesting comments from Freemasons who are interested enough in the Craft to seek out further light in Freemasonry freely in their free time by using the Internet.

As time goes by, it becomes increasingly clearer to me that many of the E-Masons with whom I come in contact are looking for something else in their Masonic journeys or even in their lives in general. At times, that "something else" has been obtaining access to information for Masonic research papers or short talks, ideas for lodge programs or fundraisers and even suggestions for the improvement on a particular process which affects a member's lodge or its candidates. Sometimes that "something else" is a camaraderie or spirit of friendship and brotherhood that the person did not find within their own lodge or within the confines of their particular religious organization. Other times, it has been the spiritual or contemplative essence of Freemasonry which has sparked the brother or sister to look for like-minded Freemasons with whom they can relate and discuss what they share in common. Lastly, I've found that E-Masonry has been a 'last hope' for some who enjoy the Craft but find their lodge meetings and functions to be insufficient to hold their attention and/or interest. This complaint largely comes from members of mainstream Masonic lodges. Why are these members losing interest?

Anecdotal evidence from years' worth of group postings makes that answer fairly easy to answer. The meetings are boring and members can find better ways to spend their valuable free time. The reading of minutes, the paying of bills, the regular announcements of blood drives and pancake breakfasts have simply become monotonous.

These members are looking for meetings the substance of which presages some deeper meaning. These members want to hear a Masonic lecture, see a degree performed or have a discussion on the symbolism of the Craft with fellow Freemasons. Freemasonry claims to be a system of moral teaching for those on a path of self-improvement. Shouldn't these things be discussed to some extent at each gathering of the lodge? Further information regarding the likes and dislikes of Freemasons from around the world are presented later in this book in what we believe to be stunning in terms of both their content and candor.

Freemasonry is an organization, but its "life" is in being a dynamic organism operating at the level of the person. Freemasonry to a dozen individual Freemasons could mean a dozen different things. Each member's concept of "My Freemasonry" is somewhat different, yet in overall terms should be equally valued. Certainly, some members are more interested and food and fellowship, while others are interested in pomp and ceremony. Others are interested in history and the association of being involved in a fraternity which boasts many notable historical individuals as members. Still others are interested in the moral teachings and/or the spiritual and contemplative nature of the mysteries of Freemasonry. It is when we combine all of the "my Freemasonry" into "Our Freemasonry" it provides that tolerance and esteem for our fellow brothers and sisters that is surely a beacon of genuine freemasonry universal.

So where do E-groups like the Masonic Light group fit into the overall scheme of things as far as Freemasonry is concerned? Do groups like Masonic Light represent the wave of the future? With cross-jurisdictional communications, emphasis on the individual and a milieu of education and the improvement that it brings, what can the Masonic jurisdictions from around the world learn from gatherings of Freemasons on the Internet? Are there lessons to be learned at all? If so, what might they be? Do the contents of the groups' discussions accurately show what it is members within a jurisdiction are interested in learning? If that is the case, to where do we go from here?

Earlier in this chapter I discussed how I had to learn about the interaction of Freemasonry with regard to recognition between various Grand Lodges or Masonic jurisdictions. I learned via the Internet! When I think of all of the countless Freemasons, many of whom are not on the Internet, I wonder if they too are blissfully ignorant of the much larger world of Freemasonry that exists outside of their own jurisdiction. Do they think that Freemasonry is pretty much the same the world over? I wonder whether they too would be amazed at what their Freemasonic brothers and sisters from around the world would have to share with them. Given the experience of running a diverse Masonic e-group, I want to continue to be a part of this grand opening-up process. Freemasons' membership numbers and participation are in substantial decline. How can the values of Freemasonry be preserved and how can we reach those who may be truly expanded as Freemasons enriched through diversity. I know of no other way to reach out other than through this book.

What started out as a project to increase my Masonic knowledge has turned out to be a much larger venture than I had ever considered. Little did I know that the Masonic Light group would be so ably and positively affect so many Freemasons around the world by sharing joy, knowledge and comfort. This is indeed a blessing.

I have also unwittingly become an advocate for the liberal Masonic community. While this was not my original intention, I accept the fact that running a large Internet discussion list, an E-community if you will, where all Freemasons are welcome to take a part, seemingly puts me into that position. Again, it is not the Masonic Light group's place to get involved in issues of Masonic recognition between jurisdictions. The group is concerned with Freemasons on the level, yes on the level, of the individual. The Working Tools, in the use of which we were instructed, can not and do not, discriminate in the hands of the honest and sincere worker.

As such, the Masonic Light group will carry on providing a place where Freemasons can discuss Freemasonry as it is practiced all over the world in a forum where each Freemason can feel welcome valued and supported . If you have Internet access and believe you would enjoy such discussion, I encourage you to join the Masonic Light Group. There is presently no cost for membership and you are under no obligation to contribute postings to the group.

The Masonic Light group is in debt to its founding members and those long serving members who have actively participated on the group for several years now. Their dedication to the Craft is demonstrated by their willingness to continue to discuss various Masonic topics, some of which are repeated from time to time for the new members, as well as their patience with the fellow members and the Group Moderator as we continue to grow as a group and further ourselves on our own Masonic pathways.

I look forward to greeting you at www.masoniclight.org.

Chapter 3
The newly discovered secrets of E-Masonry

The questionnaire - responses and comment

The decision to undertake this little study was born out of a desire to reflect upon and share our experiences as E-masons, make some sense of them and see to where they might be leading us. Both traditional Freemasonry and E-Masonry are cultural phenomena. Therefore, our enquiry had to begin with a consideration of the nature of traditional Freemasonry, the nature of the e-revolution and their current convergence. To this we would add the data collected from responses to a questionnaire designed for the purpose and then suggest how the worthy values of Freemasonry might be able to be supported albeit, in a style more adapted for the future.

From our own experience of E-Masonry, we knew that a communication medium had arrived making new types of interaction possible. E-Masonry had changed us, and we believed that it had also changed our E-Masonic colleagues. It was time to come out of the E-closet, take a look at ourselves and at the way the world was going. But, that of course begs questions on the lines of what is the nature of E-Masonry; can it be as real as Freemasonry as practised in the lodge? To belong to the Masonic Light group all you had to do was to provide your name, lodge name/number and constitution and then step into an arena of trial by peers. In more than seven years of operation there had been no organised feedback from members. Numbers had grown steadily from 50 to 705 at the time of the questionnaire and now stands at XXX. That may have an appearance of success but who knows? How do you evaluate the success of a Masonic E-group?

Obviously then, to be able to obtain a wider and more objective view of the phenomenon of E-Masonry, we needed the members to share their experiences and feelings with us. Specifically, we wanted to know from them:

(a) Is E-Masonry adding value to your Freemasonry, providing something in addition to lodge-based experience?
(b) Is E-Masonry making up for any deficiency in lodge-based provision?

That is to say, it is a core question to ascertain if E-Masonry is complementary, supplementary, both or neither with regard to any impact it may be having on traditional lodge experience. We therefore had to set questions that would tease out considered responses of both quantity and quality.

As indicated above, there is very little by way of personal data held by the ML group Moderator. Unfortunately he is not supported by a staff of either civil servants or market researchers and therefore endless data streams are not available. This questionnaire could provide a first insight into what E-Masonry might be delivering for the members of the Masonic Light group in particular and E-masonry in general.

We are so grateful to those members of ML who so kindly and thoughtfully completed and submitted answers to our online questionnaire. Indeed, with market surveys besetting us on every side we are all suffering from QSS (Questionnaire Stress Syndrome). However, we were delighted with the responses and the task is to do justice to what has been said and really make something of it. As we believe the responses are significant, we have chosen to share with the world a first glimpse of a real Masonry universal and the newly discovered secrets of E-Masonry.

We are not professional social science researchers and our methodology may not entirely match that of corporately funded academic research, but if our initial effort has identified a need for more rigorous study, then that in itself, will be regarded as a worthy achievement and outcome. However, we did set ourselves but a modest task. As previously indicated, we wanted to discuss with E-Masons how they perceived their E-Masonry in terms of (a) is it complementing the lodge experience and (b) is it making up for any deficiency in lodge-based provision. If this appears to be the case, what form might it be taking and can this provide useful support for Freemasonry in the future?

Other questions were posed around this core issue in order to build up a more complete picture. We were particularly interested to know what feelings, if any, there may be towards Freemasons with whom the only interaction was by E-communication, how satisfactory, or otherwise, it was proving to be and yet could become.

Also, we specifically asked about attendance and participation as we were anxious to detect if E-Masonry was proving to be a distraction from traditional Masonic contribution to lodges. If we had found that the responses indicated low levels of attendance and participation, we would have looked to see if this was attributable to, and a reflection of, apathy in general or indicative of an intrusion by E-Masonry in particular. If it was found to be the case that E-Masonry was causing a decline in attendance and participation, there could be some consideration of what, if anything could or should be done about it. We specifically asked the question pertaining to challenges to traditional Freemasonry, again to tease out if E-Masonry could help out or be perceived as a threat.

The responses provided by members of the Masonic Light Group have provided a base of very interesting revealing data and it is to this that we will now turn. Hopefully it will be possible to detect trends, areas of consensus and obtain some clear guidance on what ways, if any, E-Masonry may be able to support Freemasonry in the future. It would appear from the responses that there may be more than 40 different Masonic E-groups and obviously we would not claim to have any idea of what they all have to offer. Our data and therefore our observations and conclusions are confined to that derived from the Masonic Light group, with its broad diversity of members from so many different jurisdictions; but, with the proviso that the responses may reflect the experience and values of other E-groups. However, we take the view that it is unlikely that the culture of the Masonic Light Group is substantially different from that of any other E-group, but on this we could be wrong.

Question 1. Gender:

The gender breakdown of ML is a known and therefore there was a desire to see if male/female response matched the composition of the group. Secondly, there was a wish to see if there was any significant difference between male and female responses.

Response:

Total 112: Male 105 out of 675 = 5.6%   Female 7 of 30 = 23.3%

The total number of responses was by 15.9% of the group. Our initial, and yes perhaps residual reaction, is one of some disappointment. After over six years of service, the ML group moderator made a personal appeal to members to help out in this way and perhaps more could and should have contributed. There is a view that in this life there are participants and spectators, initially, at least, it would have perhaps been thought that Freemasonry would have appealed to those of a more participatory inclination. However, further consideration of this will be deferred until there is a later examination of the responses to the question devoted to issues of participation.

No one complained that the questionnaire was unwarranted or intrusive; to the contrary, many of the responses were clearly undertaken with enthusiasm some providing their names or clear indications of their identity although, of course, this was something for which we did not ask. However, we are quite certain that we have data of quality and use and the positive nature of the responses was very encouraging.

The difference between the percentages of male and female respondents may not be overly significant. From the jurisdictions indicated it would appear that the female responses are all from branches of Co-Masonry and none are members of female-only lodges. Further, from the responses it is clear that they are 100% for a greater recognition of diversity within Freemasonry in general and with the clear priority to achieve a substantially increased level of recognition of Co-Masonry in particular. Otherwise, there does not appear to be any other significant differences, by gender, in the substance or style of the responses.

Perhaps female Freemasons see E-Masonry as a major vehicle for the alteration of mindsets within mainstream jurisdictions with this leading to greater inclusion and achieving wider parameters for "official" recognition, visitation and communication. Answers to subsequent questions indicate that by virtue of its cross-jurisdictional operation, the Masonic Light group has challenged traditional patterns of thought and understanding. It remains to be seen if this will ascend the rungs of the hierarchical ladders and to where, if anywhere, this might lead. With only just over 4% of its membership female, perhaps the ML Group should seek to increase female representation.

Question 2 Age

Joining members are not asked about their age. We wanted to see if the age range of the respondents matched that of the perceived age profile of masons in general.

(See: Table 1 at the conclusion of the book)

As it is not deemed necessary for the Moderator to ask for age details from joining members, there is no way of knowing if the age profile of the respondents images that of the whole group.

That over 48% of the respondents were in the age range 40 – 60 does seem to suggest some symmetry with actual lodge attendance rather than the whole of lodge membership. The understanding is that the average age of Freemasons is between the mid to late fifties; if that is correct and the sample is representative of the whole group, it may be the case that the membership of the Masonic Light group is of a younger age range than an average lodge. It should come as no surprise if that is true and indicative of the more than 40 putative Masonic e-groups.

That Freemasonry appears to be unable to appeal to significant numbers of younger people is a cause of angst among jurisdictional leadership with central overheads in general and lodge secretaries with unsustainable income levels in particular. The reasons why Freemasonry is not attracting younger people, we would suggest, may be something on the lines of insufficient resonation, engagement or connection between the traditional practice and presentation of Freemasonry with the aspirations of the generation that that the grand lodges are seeking to attract – they simply do not touch.

What might be of greater concern than the rates of recruitment is that the average length of membership may be between five and ten years, and perhaps nearer five than ten and heading south. Obviously, if retention rates could be significantly improved that would proportionately remove the pressures for recruitment. However, unlike in the world of corporate employment, recruitment into Freemasonry does not require an investment by the organisation; the costs are accommodated by the joining member. Retention may require investment. It may be easier to perpetuate cycles of recruitment than to provide real longer term engagement at lodge level: but at what additional cost?

What then are the contemporary cultural mores in terms of the work ethic, education, citizenship, religiosity, fraternity, charity and gender of the second generation post World War II people? How divergent are they from the traditional values of

Freemasonry are they, if at all; is it a matter of style or substance, or both; can ubiquitous E-communication help?

3. Jurisdiction:

(Also known as Constitution, Obedience or Grand Lodge.) Freemasonry is universally spread over the globe, but it is not a monolithic entity. Freemasonry is "divided" over the globe in locally based jurisdictions. Each of these jurisdictions embodies the accidents of its birth and other local events as they have since occurred. Most are precious about their prerogative over matters of eligibility for membership and the recognition, or otherwise, of other jurisdictions. It must be the case that you cannot have an organisation without an organisation. That being said, we wished to see if there were detectable trends between jurisdictions and the responses made. We have already identified that the responses from the Co-Masonic jurisdictions were clearer than any others about the desire for their Freemasonry to be recognised as practicing "regular" Freemasonry and their members to be recognized as Freemasons without prejudice.

On the Masonic Light group there is representation from a staggering 150 jurisdictions! There is also no consistency of recognition; that is to say Jurisdiction A recognises Jurisdiction B and C, but, Jurisdiction B recognises Jurisdiction A but not C! ML recognises them all. In Table 1 we show the main responses by jurisdiction.

(See: Table 2 at the conclusion of the book)

Whilst the Table shows that five jurisdictions had a response rate that was significantly in excess of their representation on ML, it cannot be said that any jurisdictions in particular dominated the responses. This mirrors the fact that no jurisdiction dominates the E-mail traffic on Masonic Light. Of the twenty most represented jurisdictions with 493 members, only three, with 77 members are not from the USA. Indeed, of the 150 jurisdictions represented, more than ninety are USA based. However, that does not make for conformity or monochromatic style or substance, far from it. The diversity of these jurisdictions ensures lively and multi-faceted debate and usually passionate exchanges. Comments about the extent of diversity, even within jurisdictions, were made in response to later questions.

Questions 4/5/6 Length of Masonic service/ length of E-Masonry service/number of e-groups joined.

The anxieties about Freemasonry's future are encapsulated in the recruitment/retention debate. We wished to obtain an impression of how E-Masonry might be assisting, or hindering the Masonic membership numbers. Perhaps the number of E-groups to which members belonged might be in indication of the quantitative impact of E-Masonry. We would be taking this with Q14/15 looking to see how this may compare with lodge attendance and responsibilities.

(See: Tables 3, 4 & 5 at the conclusion of the book)

If it is the case that the average duration of Masonic service is between five and ten years, it can be seen the sample does not concur, its average is nearer twenty years. In considering the average duration of Masonic service, we touched on the issue of retention. If it is taken that E-Masonry has been operative for roughly ten years, is it possible that it has helped to retain an interest in Freemasonry? We don't know. We didn't have the temerity, to ask. But, if the average service of Freemasons on E-groups is greater than those who were not, it does leave open the possibility that E-Masonry is material to their retention and interest. To demonstrate this, further specific research would be necessary before conclusions could be drawn other than, of course, that it could perhaps be inferred that it is unlikely that E-Masonry has been an impediment to retention.

Additionally, we wanted to know how long our members had been operative Masons; again assuming that E-Masonry has been operative for about ten years it was of particular interest to see for those, who had been Freemasons for less than eleven years how, how long they had been E-Masons. In Table 6 below, we have listed 4 against 5 and 6 for those who had been in Freemasonry for less than eleven years.

(See: Table 6 at the conclusion of the book)

Sixty of the respondents, 55.5% had been in Freemasonry for less than eleven years. For most of these people then, it is the case that E-Masonry has accompanied their formative Masonic years. That is to say, they have been nurtured on both the traditional fare and any cuisine nuevo that E-Masonry may be bringing. Is it possible that they could be "normal" Freemasons with traditional received views on the "jurisdiction" of their Jurisdiction, limited perceptions of universality and diversity, the reality of Masonic progress, restrictions on visiting etc? We will see if the responses that the above group subsequently make, are significantly different from those for whom E-Masonry has arrived at a much later stage in their Masonic experience. That is to say, do old habits die hard?

That 47% of the respondents were in more than three e-groups and that 18% were in more than six egroups came as somewhat of a surprise although, we do not know much about these groups, their size or their specific purpose. Some answered or qualified their response by saying that they were in too many! We had to keep reminding ourselves that the comments we had received, in response to the questionnaire, did not necessary apply, in whole or in part, to the Masonic Light Group alone. Certainly there are different Masonic E-groups that are organized to serve specific purposes or to focus on specific aspects of Freemasonry. What is possibly inferred by these responses is that the respondents' individual lodges and jurisdictions may not be satisfying their appetite for Masonic study and instruction.

Perhaps the number of E-groups to which members belonged might also be in indication of an impact on traditional support for the local lodge. This would be considered and compared with the later questions pertaining to lodge attendance and responsibilities.

Q7 Positive Aspects of E-Masonry

As indicated, we wanted to know from E-Masons themselves what they perceived, as individuals, were the benefits of E-Masonry. There was the temptation to provide a tick-list of possible answers but notwithstanding the inherent difficulty of people saying the same thing but in many different ways or, meaning different things but using similar wording we left the response open. It seemed that the responses obtained fell into the four broad categories of:

Universality	95%,
Masonic knowledge	56%
Practicalities	12%
Personal Masonic advancement	9%

The numbers reflect more than one choice.

Responses:

Yes   No

A: Yes

Universal/worldwide	(46)*
Broader/different points of view	(9)*
Cross-jurisdiction	(32)**
Diversity	(22)
Meeting brothers from around the world	(1)
Chance to build global family	(1)

*This does not entail cross-jurisdiction communication

** This response is understated. On nearly all forms a positive view on cross-jurisdiction communication was indicated within the responses to subsequent questions. The few that were negative to cross-jurisdictional communication did so with what was undoubtedly indications of varying degrees of regret.

It is the case that with these responses we obtained far more than we anticipated. From this point on, there does seem to be a significant challenge to some of the traditional Masonic rhetoric; none more so than the notion of "universality".

Universality:

To discover the existence of masons from other worlds.

Helped me to realise the true universality of Freemasonry

Within rituals, great celebration is made of the globalisation of Freemasonry. But of course emperors, kings and religious leaders; and since then, political theorists, labour movements and capitalism have had and still have global visions and aspirations. Perhaps there is persuasive logic about a one world. Perhaps, as never before, has the spirit of the age been so "universal" and globalism is a great thing, as long as everyone shares our values. Perhaps we all wish to recreate man in our own image. We do not know if the quest for universalism, as clearly indicated in the responses received, indicates the perspective of E-Masonry in general or Masonic Light in particular. The latter is perhaps more likely given that cross-jurisdictional recognition is a tenet of the group. But, as water covers two thirds of the globe and e-communication covers that and the rest, until proven otherwise, we take the view that E-Masonry, by virtue of the nature of the medium, has an implicit value of universality that transcends that of any one ritual book or jurisdictional regulation.

However, it is only in thirty-two of the more than one-hundred responses in which cross-jurisdictional communication is explicitly celebrated. But it is clear from responses to further questions that there is a much more significant aspiration to breakdown jurisdictional barriers albeit to different extents and in different degrees; for different reasons and to achieve different outcomes. However, several jurisdictions have lodges around the globe and E-groups are a way of engaging with the totality of the jurisdiction of which one is a member. More specifically, a jurisdictionally based E-group could operate without involvement from deemed irregular or unrecognised jurisdictions.

From the responses and postings received there was a celebration of the diversity of different jurisdictions but for some, through E-Masonry, there were levels of diversity detected, within single jurisdictions, that had been hitherto unrealised,. Also, for some other jurisdictions there was a realisation that other recognised jurisdictions had levels of diversity much greater than formerly and generally understood. The respondents made clear that they were far more in an appreciation of Freemasonry universal than before they had E-communication. Whilst in answer to the question pertaining to the universality of Freemasonry, we would like at this point to share what one respondent wrote, *"With over fifty years as a Freemason, I have discovered things about the craft that I never dreamed existed."* The whole of the response makes quite clear that it was an enlightening and pleasing discovery of differences and diversity in a new paradigm of Freemasonry universal.

B: The study of nature and science

Exchanging/sharing ideas	**(24)**
Source of knowledge/education	**(22)**
New ideas/information	**(9)**
Thought provoking	**(1)**
New insights	**(2)**
Keeping up to date	**(2)**

Comradely communication across different groups and among people who it is unlikely would have ever met. A larger pool of knowledge to draw from.

Helped me think re-think; helped me search and ask questions.

Masonic knowledge: For us, Masonic Light has provided a consistent flow of Masonic knowledge, ideas, insights and interpretations and that alone has justified the formation of the group and our support for it since its formation. Also, and in the tradition of Enlightenment Freemasonry, there has been a succession of valued academic knowledge, certainly counting as the study of nature and science, from professors, experts and specialists in their chosen subjects. Sixty respondents referred to the educational value of E-Masonry. The books the members suggest for reading, quotations and internet links are of a magnitude and diversity with which no one lodge or jurisdiction could possibly compete. As one respondent wrote, *"Differing opinions from differing backgrounds are expressed giving you the feeling that you have heard several sides of an issue before deciding what you think."* On a later question asking if people were active in their lodges, we didn't ask what they were doing but, many indicated the nature of their activity – that 32 respondents were lodge lecturers/educationalists is hardly a surprise. In fact it might well be suggested that if people are giving Masonic lectures, unless they are fulltime professional researchers, or connected to something like the Masonic Light group, there may be good reasons to worry about the quality and relevance of the material being disseminated – like, where is the stuff coming from?

There is no doubt that the Masonic Light group over its seven years has been blessed with enough able minds to make their contributions alone, sufficient for group membership. Whilst the "lurkers" pose a conundrum, there has been enough intellectually stimulating dialogue to perhaps understand the "lurkers" as being "baskers" in Masonic Light. Many respondents thanked the Moderator for enabling such an outstanding resource of Masonic knowledge, some said that the group is overwhelmingly their source of Masonic knowledge and some said that the Moderator will never know just how many Freemasons have benefited, how much knowledge has been disseminated during the last seven years and the great good that has surely been achieved as a result.

Given that Freemasonry is no more and no less than a template to make sense of this earthly life, it is not surprising that issues other than the origins of Freemasonry, the transition from operative to speculative and what are we going to do about declining membership numbers, are discussed. The ML group advertises that it is a forum to discuss all topics that pertain to Masonry, from the exoteric to the esoteric. It is the case that the corpus of New Age History, Roslyn Chapel, Rennes Le Chateau, the marital status of Jesus and so many others are recurring "threads" as older members have new thoughts or ideas and newer members raise the issues enabling a refresh round of consideration. Not Masonic topics you say? Members will tell you otherwise. These conversations take place in the midst of more elementary aspects of the Craft, such as discussions on working tools, fundraisers and other lodge programs.

Occasionally, long-time members do say, "Haven't we discussed this before?" and complain of, *Members who do not lurk for a while before posting and/or read and review the message archives to see if their interests have been covered already.* But issues worthy of consideration once are usually worthy of repetition. Also, it is not as if the problems arising from these issues have actually been resolved to the satisfaction of all: therefore the group is always open to new ideas and research on topics old or new. Even ML can not claim to have resolved all of life's mysteries. There are people on the group who have published books that are of interest to group members and who contribute to the message threads as well. And, if they want to promote their latest book, that is not a problem, providing it has some relationship to Freemasonry. There is evidence in the postings that Freemasons have joined Masonic Light and that the discussion and diversity of their ideas have altered long held perspectives of Masonic understanding. Some have indicated that they would know nothing had it not been for E-Masonry. But it is not all minds and intellect, people shall not live by logic alone, other aspects of our personalities have also been touched.

C: Daily Masonic Advancement

Good for the growth of Freemasonry **(2)**
Self improvement **(2)**
Brotherly love, relief and truth
Brotherly love
Making friends
Companionship
Meeting like minded individuals
Communities of brethren can develop who share particular interests
Sense of belonging when unable to attend lodge
Teaches toleration

The ML group is not just a virtual group of unknown members – it's real. The relationship is also real on all possible levels. It is a rather exceptional opportunity to communicate with the world on such reliable terms.
Having international friends who appear to be having the same joys and sorrows as freemasons as we do here at home.

Masonic personal advancement: Some, considering petitioning for acceptance into Freemasonry, are told that it is only five or seven nights a year; that may well be an understatement. There are infinite Masonic "attractions" to occupy five nights a week, every week, if there is the appetite and personal circumstances permit. Also, the weekends can be filled too. But we take the view that Freemasonry is primarily about personal improvement that is manifested by good works at work, home and all of life. We find the cliché, Freemasonry is "to make good men better", quite possibly, disgusting and this is discussed in Parts 1 and 4. Freemasonry we believe is for any person who wishes to become better able to serve humanity. But, before there can be a soundly functioning social skill-set, there must be an apposite mind-set. The Masonic ethic requires a personal daily Masonic advancement.

If Masonic input is only obtained from lodge meetings attended a handful of times a year or if attendance at lodge meetings does not provide anything like Masonic advancement, then there is certainly Masonic malnutrition. One respondent wrote that because of Masonic E-communication, "*I actively think about Freemasonry every day not just a couple of times a month*". When taken with the response that the ML group provides, "*Philosophic content that helps us grow as human beings and become better people,* then we must realise that we are standing on some sort of "holy" ground. It may well be the case that there are in the world people, who are better Freemasons for being E-Masons and that the world is a better place for them and their contribution. Respectfully, one is reminded of the Biblical quotation, "My word shall not return unto void but shall accomplish the thing whereunto it is sent." Light will dispel darkness. In being a contributory E-Mason, lives around the world are being touched. *Light, "sunlight" that is all colours.*

D: Practicalities

Speedy/rapid/prompt/quick	**(8)**
Information when we can't attend lodge	**(1)**
Wide range of opinions that you would be able to get in a real-life lodge	**(1)**
Cost effective	**(1)**
Not having to travel	**(1)**

E-Masonry embodies the contemporary concept of 24/7, the Temple that never sleeps. Its greatest practicality is that it provides the member with the opportunity to practice Freemasonry at times that can be planned around commitments, responsibilities; to suit convenience and without detriment to family, self or other connections. It enables rapid responses to questions ranging from Masonic history and the meaning of life to receiving cosmological queries on the juxtaposition of planets and their allusions to certain of our degrees, as well as information on guided trips around Grand Lodge, Great Queen Street, London, UK. The book lists and web references provided do at times constitute information overload for some, but they are grist to the mill for others. Comments about information being available when lodge attendance isn't possible, cost efficiency and avoiding the need to travel were within the responses to this question. But they were not extensive. However, in the consideration of later questions, the practicalities of E-Masonry are more fully indicated.

It has been most warm when members have indicated that when planning travel to another part of the world, they are able at the speed of light, to find Freemasons and lodges just waiting to welcome them, *Making connections throughout the world to assist with visitation or personal needs.* Looking at responses to later questions we will see just how the practicalities of e-communication can be effective and sometimes life changing.

Q8 Any downsides of E-Masonry

Obviously, we wanted know if there were aspects of E-Masonry that were unhelpful, or worse, may militate against the benefits of E-Masonry.

Responses:

A: Yes/No

Yes	**81**
No	**14***

* 3 were qualified by reference to the delete key – the most widely used key in E-mail – to denote that many email messages shared with the group were insufficient to engage time or attention.

Most respondents indicated areas of some negativity. We have divided the responses into four categories: inherent, behavioural and quality of content. Inevitably, there is some overlap.

B: Unsatisfactory – inherent?

- Anonymity of lurkers
- Difficulty accessing web links to sites included in postings
- Negative behaviours presenting negative image to non-masons
- Internet Service Provider failures
- Lack of communication disciplines/email conventions
- Bar room/chat room style of communication
- Communications cold because of the medium
- Can't hear emotions/body language
- Censorship
- Bad grammar/spelling
- Time consuming
- Saying things in email that you wouldn't say in person
- Too much traffic / Too much information / Too many messages
- Not meeting face to face
- Time to root out gems from garbage
- Communication with non-recognised masons
- Not able to really get to know other participants.
- Unnecessary credentials and postnomial posting
- Signing-off without name or jurisdiction

System failures and difficulties accessing links are just the facts of E-life and we all really do hope and believe that the product will become even more reliable than it already is. Communication with non-recognised Freemasons we do not regard as a problem of E-Masonry per se, it is a matter of E-group selection and management. If a group is formed on the principle of cross-jurisdictional recognition, it is for those Freemasons who are so disposed. If it the case that a really helpful E-group has degrees of recognition that may pose issues for some Freemasonic con-sciences and preference, then it is individual decision time. This issue is more fully discussed in responses to the question in-cluded for this very purpose.

Some respondents complained of the lack of communica-tion disciplines and e-mail, conventions, use of chat room style, bad grammar and spelling. We are not sure if there is in exist-ence an authoritive consensus on how E-group communica-tion should be undertaken. Some messages are undertaken in haste and by those with limited keyboard skills, some after a generous nightcap, English for many is not their first language and it would seem that there exists many and interesting ver-sions of the English language! Respondents referred to the use of unnecessary credentials at one extreme and signing-off with-out name or jurisdiction at the other. Again, protocols need time to evolve and gain a consensus. A balance will need to be cre-ated between unnecessary levels of formality and unacceptable levels of flippancy. The seven liberal arts and sciences we are urged to study and it would be helpful to demonstrate their in-fluence when participating in E-Masonry. For better or worse, one's grammatical, rhetorical and logical skills are predomi-nantly on display. Participating in E-communication can cer-tainly help one to improve in those areas in general and in particular.

Someone complained of the *anonymity of the "lurkers"*, an interesting comment. A respondent wrote, "*Occasionally it seems difficult to find a niche in E-Masonry, to get to know other masons via the E-mail especially if one tends to lurk more than respond to posts.*" If each member of the group communicated regularly, the E-mail traffic would be unsustainable and unmanageable. It would support those who commented that the traffic was already excessive and that it was time-consuming to sort out *"the gems from the garbage"*. We take the view that sustainable E-Masonry requires highly developed editorial skills and we shall return to this gift in subsequent discussion.

There were responses indicating that because of the medium, the communication is cold, there is an inability to hear emotions or read body language, not being able to meet face to face, *"…not being able to see a smile properly in letters or get to know other members."* These are seriously minority views, they do not concur with our experience of ML nor with the majority of responses received. These are discussed below in consideration of the question set for this purpose.

The view that there are communications in E-mail that would not be said in person is interesting. Hopefully, it is true as there have been some exchanges on Email which in the flesh may have had disastrous consequences. Fortunately these are few and far between and raise issues pertaining to the group moderator's role in the discussions and the potential of the calming influence of other members. In reply to this question we received this answer: *"Not really, the occasional and sometimes bitter disagreements often serve to bring out the best in some of the other members of a list as they step forward to resolve conflicts while endeavouring to maintain a manageable level of fraternal decorum."*

E-Masonry provides access and freedoms hitherto unimagined, the culture will need to develop and norms will need time to mature and become established. But let us be clear, this is a medium for self-regulation and personal responsibility. It is an arena for judgement by ones peers and it will soon become apparent if a person's contributions generate no response, they will die the death of a thousand delete keys. However, there are times when E-behaviour is unacceptable to some members of the group.

C: Unsatisfactory – style of communication behavior

Many different negative, even pejorative terms were used to describe the style of some E-communications. This included 24 references to unacceptable intolerance towards:- other jurisdictions, religions, ideas and female Freemasons. The remainder of the descriptions can be summarised as: non-Masonic, chauvinistic, ad hominem, acrimonious, disrespectful, contentious and egotistical.

Indeed, time is of the essence: and so also is timing. The distribution of the questionnaires coincided with one of the heavier E-Mail exchanges in ML's history. It had thundered on for over two weeks with a weight of contributions, counter-contributions, intolerant comments, emotive language and language of questionable civility. This sort of behaviour does occur from time to time. Imagine adult Freemasons speaking to one another and behaving as if they were teenagers on the playground. When in E-communication with people from around the globe, it is good advice to be extra careful with the use of colloquialisms and humour. It is quite easy to offend. As stated previously, these occasions do sometimes bring out the best in some group members as well as the group Moderator. We guessed this perhaps had not been the most appropriate occasion or best time for introspection: but, perhaps this was as bad as it was going to get, lessons were learned and it will only get better. Also, we may be reacting in an over-sensitive way. Perhaps, some of the E-Masonry negatives were not directed at ML at all, but with other E-groups ML members may also belong to.

A respondent wrote, *"Unfortunately you come across intolerance and bigotry within masonry. In "real" it is easy to just not visit the lodge, in E-masonry the posts are there in your face."* Three of the 22 who said that there were no downsides to E-Masonry did refer to the delete key; perhaps they are more accomplished E-Masons. For some on the group, Freemasonry is important as it provides a framework to make sense of the world, is a basis for values and for self-respect. Much of the material on ML has been highly emotive, regardless of on which side of the divide a person may stand. Views on issues such as females and ethnic minorities in Freemasonry, its position vis-à-vis the major religions, pantheism, gnosticism and atheism; political divides past and present, all can be raised, promoted and defended with passion. There have been a significant number of instances where genuine misunderstandings have occurred, but as is often the case, heat was generated before the light was finally allowed to shine in. Perhaps when an apology is made, progress has also been made. It has been very disappointing however when, in the first instance, the goodwill of another has been doubted.

A principle characteristic of ML is that of tolerance. Basically anything outside of rude and/or inflammatory language is tolerated, indeed every thing is tolerated except intolerance itself. A respondent said, *"The e-mail medium allows people to hide and act unseemly at times. It is tough to stay abreast of all the threads and some minds are not open or tolerant."* Perhaps it is necessary to make very clear to joining members what the values of the particular E-group are and for the other members to protect them. The way forward may not be, in the first instance, the use of the awesome and arbitrary power of a group Moderator to wipe out a persons E-existence. If people are suffering from inflammation, let's try some healing. One of the group's most valuable and popular contributors was requested to have a brief spell of non-contribution. During this time off-group communication was maintained and E-Masons and E-Masonry thereby grew in stature.

D: Unsatisfactory – quality of content

Negative words were used about the content of some communications. These can be summarised as: Unworthy topics, irrelevant, lack intellectual discipline, tedious, and unoriginal, using the medium for complaints about lodge/jurisdiction and members having specific agendas and turning every thread (discussion topic) to the aforesaid agenda.

Comments about communications being irrelevant, lacking in intellectual discipline or being unoriginal require some un-picking. Again, the declared purpose of any particular E-group must be considered. If a Masonic E-group is fortunate enough to have science professors among its membership and he or she contributes pieces that constitute genuine knowledge and learn-ing, it will be of interest to most open minds. Or, if not of par-ticular interest, then the openness of the mind will allow that it may be of interest to other group members. Discussions among American members about seriously regional cuisine may not in the first instance be thought to be of interest of Masonic stu-dents in Beirut. But if the communications are undertaken with style and careful humour, they will have an entertainment value; again, style and humour will appeal to an open mind. But for the really busy and more narrowly focussed, then for the threads such as "black-eyed peas", the delete button is always there, al-though the view could be taken that life is too short not to take the opportunity to gain insight into other cultures. This is not to say that food is discussed as a topic of conversation, "belly-masons" aside, the food reference is used merely to illustrate the point.

The comment about lacking intellectual discipline is of in-terest. On an E-group there will be people at various levels of intellectual attainment and ability. Indeed, if there is a reality at all, is it not contained within various levels of meaning and sym-bol? Some questions and contributions will appear to some to be elementary, but the idea that people can join E-groups and progress through grades must be an encouraging concept. It would shape the tone and temper of contributions and minimise the use of negative communication styles as discussed above.

The response decrying the use of the medium for complaints about one's lodge or jurisdiction is interesting. It may be cathar-tic gaining the sympathy of other members. They may be able to learn from negative experiences and in answer to another ques-tion a respondent wrote of the benefit of, *"..having international friends who appear to be having the same joys and sorrows as freemasons as we do here at home".*

We were surprised that 14 respondents said that as far they were concerned there was nothing unsatisfactory with E-Masonry. We would not necessarily concur. Who were these people? Were they young in age, in Masonic and E- experience? Table 7 indicates that is not necessarily the case.

(See: Tables 7 at the conclusion of the book)

The sample of 14 with an average age of 51 years, 13 in Freemasonry and 4.6 in E-Masonry does not seem to indicate an immature set.

E-Masonry is an extraordinary example of the dialectic of freedom and responsibility. Very few of us who use it have any real idea of the scale or scope of resource beneath the index fingers of both hands. With E-Masonry, we can grow and mature in ways hitherto undreamt. Abused it can hurt, damage or even destroy. We have to realise the reality and vitality of the medium. This is further indicated that E-Masonry is "flesh and blood", that cyber-space is within the paradigm of space and time and therefore the communication must be for promoting the good in individuals in particular and for promoting the good of humankind in general.

Q9 Level of affinity with other E-Masons with whom they had not met.

Yes, this was an attempt to tease out how members might be feeling about each other. Did they feel that the other members were "flesh and blood", real people and that through E-Masonry alone there could be a degree of relationship that was satisfactory and had a useful role.

Response:

A: Yes/No

Yes **78**
No **14**

B: Yes, Its basis

The common interest made for a common bond (20)

Had gained respect for the knowledge and /or character of other members as demonstrated through E-communication. (18)

Would like to meet members. (10)

Had met up and/or made firm friendships (8)

Believed that they had acquired insight into member's personalities/characters. (5)

"A number of people I have communication with I feel I have an affinity with and this is strange when one has not met face to face."

"There are several I have never laid eyes on but I feel like I know them."

"I really do think that all of us believe that we have a relationship that is more than E-link".
"It is sort of like going to the pub and running into a group of friends and interesting people."

C: No and why

"Often impersonal e-mails."

"I do not feel that way"

"Unfortunately not really, I can know their opinions on certain aspects, but that is not to say that I truly know or understand them, that is in the absence of meeting them."

"I have never met a stranger in a lodge or Masonic gathering."

We are not psychologists, but we do have feelings. People meet in shared physical space and time, whether at home work or play and time and have shared experiences.

Sometimes lasting friendships are formed, however most people are soon forgotten. With many of the people that we meet, they have no apparent impact on our lives, we are as but ships passing in the night. *"If it were not for these lists I would be less of a human and less of a mason."* Is it not the case that much in human relationships is based on the benefits of cooperation and that in many walks of life it is a case of use and be used? Is there anything wrong with that, especially when times are for better?

Perhaps the test is what happens when times are for worse, when a person's use is limited and they need more out than they can put back in. Oscar Wilde, when being told that we are here on this earth to help others asked, "And what then are the others here for?" Perhaps it is the case that relationships do grow to such an extent that for whatever reasons, communications continue even though there may not be much advantage to all of the parties involved. But, the ability to contribute has much to do with the endowed gifts of nature and nurture. The realisation that these are endowed must be a basis for the exercise of compassion and support.

Some people are but a voice on the other end of a telephone or pen-friends, but this may be important communication and these people may be important people and recognised as people, although not seen. *"You treat it like a blind person, in that you cannot see them, but you get a sense for what they are about."* Often, when people meet after engaging in frequent telephone conversations it is said that it is good to put a face to a voice. *"I recognised a name when I was introduced to a brother from another lodge – we instantly hit it off, because we were both members here."*

Is it not sometimes said that we have met a person but do not know them? *"I know more about some E-masons I haven't met in person than those from my own lodge. It's simply due to more communication and sharing."* Could that really be true of Freemasons with whom we sit in lodge – going through the motions of communication and relationships? *"How well do we know those with whom we sit in lodge with a few times a year? It's possible in many cases there is more meaningful/genuine communication on "E" than in the flesh."*

While we agree with the majority on this question, we were astonished at the responses given and that the membership largely feels the same way! Seventy-eight respondents indicated that they, through E-Masonry alone, had created an affinity with other Freemasons even though they had not met them in "the flesh".

These are stunning comments and we do not claim to have anything like a full understanding of them in their present context, their implications or their future potential. We, from our own experience, can only concur with them. There are E-Masons in the group that chose to share with the group that they had suffered a serious setback of some sort; we seriously shared their pain. Similarly, when members have chosen to share with us their joy, Masonic or otherwise, we have celebrated with them. ML members have lived the horror of losing a child to the joy of adopting babies from poor countries. Indeed, we have wept both tears of joy and pain for all involved.

We are humbled by these comments and we do not know what to say other than to repeat our belief that we are standing on some sort of holy ground. In our conclusions later, we will attempt to provide an initial and tentative indication of what we believe may be the force of these comments, their possible implications and how they might be developed for the good of Freemasonry in general and for individual Freemasons in particular.

Q10 Satisfactory relationships through E-Masonry alone.

Assuming that there might be some positive response to Q9 above, this question extends towards a largely unthinkable; that is to say, sounding out the concept of stand alone E-Masonry being a satisfactory form of Freemasonry. We were not expecting a significant Yes vote.

Responses:

A: Yes/No - Unqualified

Yes **40** No **47**

"Yes indeed, I think cultural and political change can start here."

"Sure hope so –given the dismal state of the alternative."

B: Qualified responses - 23

Yes but not a complete relationship
Yes may be only possibility for some (2)
Yes, but personal contact is better
More or less, yes

No, more than yes
Not really, not altogether, no

Possibly (6)
Don't know

Unclear question

"Yes, but I feel more on the surface than in depth. Masons cannot live in a virtual world, our work must be real. Also the purpose of this list, like craft, is not to make friends nor to socialise but to learn, work and advance for the good of humanity."

"Not totally. Nothing can replace a lodge, but you learn how they think."

We were astonished that 40 respondents, without qualification, indicated that they believed that E-Masonry could, on a stand alone basis, be an acceptable form of Freemasonry. John McEnro's immortal line came to mind, "You cannot be serious!" But we have every to reason to believe that these are serious responses; they are supported with appropriate comment and may impact on how Freemasonry is practised in the future.

Respondents indicated the value of E-Masonry for those, who by reason of working in remote places or evening hours, do not have access to lodge meetings. Similarly, it was suggested that E-Masonry might be suitable for older and infirm Freemasons, but this raises issues. It is our belief that E-Masonry should be a medium of choice and not imposed as a substitute for visiting if that hitherto, has been the practice within the lodge and jurisdiction. On the other hand effectively visiting people who are chronically sick, traumatised or bereaved is a highly charged task requiring a very humane mindset and perhaps a professional skill-set.

In **Table 6** we showed details from 60 responses from Freemasons of less than eleven years of service. Their responses to this question were a definite 16 Yes and definite 26 No. Had the majority decided definitely Yes, the view could have been taken that the data was skewed by their inexperience. What is the case is that 25 respondents with <u>over</u> 10 years Masonic service, 20% of the total sample, were of the view that satisfactory Masonic relationships could be established and maintained through E-Masonry alone!

Seventeen of the respondents found the question challenging and their qualified answers show evidence of deliberation. Yet, and on the other hand, many of the Yes answers and No answers were accompanied by an exclamation mark. It seemed to be a question, unlike no other in this set, with an even scale of divide between Yes and No and Not sure. We are also saying yes and no and that we are not sure. However in our closing remarks we will suggest some possible ways of taking forward some of the energy indicated in the responses.

Q11 Does E-Masonry complement or supplement traditional Freemasonry.

This for us was intended to be the core question. We wanted to know if E-Masonry was adding value, making up for perceived deficiencies or something of both. This was to provide the substance of the Questionnaire. We got it nearly right; that is to say, we got it wrong. It would have been better to have expressed this as two questions viz. (1) Does E-Masonry add anything to Freemasonry as is; and (2) does E-Masonry make up for any limitations in Freemasonry as is. This lack of clarity means that we have not got as clear an idea from the members as we would have liked about E-Masonry complementing and/or supplementing traditional lodge-based practice. The difference may be important; activities that complement the lodge should not be perceived as a threat, supplementary activities might be an indication of a challenge to the status quo.

A: Yes/No/Don't know

Yes	89
No	2
Don't know	11
Not yet	1

B: Yes

52 <u>for Knowledge/information/ideas/education</u>.

"In lodge they don't want to talk about morals, symbology or eso-teric. On the lists, the members come awake for these topics. I believe that the lists are allowing Freemasonry to bloom again; we can talk to like-minded all over the world."

"Better communication, better information at a lower cost."

26 <u>for broadening/diversifying/revitalising masonry</u>.

"This is open 24/7; my lodge meets five times a year. Without E-lists, I doubt I'd make the daily advancement in Masonic knowl-edge as well or as easily as I have done."

5 <u>enabling Masonic contact when you can not attend lodge</u>.

"Soon we may be able to open meetings via video conferencing."

2 <u>enabling meeting with other masons</u>

"E-Masonry already complements the lodge experience for me, but the facilitation of being able to meet so many brethren and sisters from around the world is a masonry I would not otherwise have. The only thing better for me would be the ability to sit in open lodge with them. I realise that, because of my obligations, I could not sit in open lodge with them."

"E-Masonry provides an opportunity to expand the fellowship aspect of the local lodge and provides a basis for comparative ma-sonry."

2 <u>enabling talking freely</u>

"I see it as a tool for masons to seek more light. This is not a place for GLs to meddle in."

B: No

That two people said No is a surprise; again, perhaps this reflects how poorly the question was set. We do not know much about other E-groups but, it is difficult to believe that any participant on Masonic Light can fail to receive some Masonic additionality.

"Serious discussion on this forum can be carried forth to lodge and discussed further. This would serve to expose non-members to universal thinking that may be stifled in the local environment. Show them the farm."

"E-Masonry is definitely not a replacement, but it complements the lodge, providing an interface apart from the Masonic experience in the lodge."

"It provides regular daily contact with masons we would otherwise never meet."

"Not yet, but within a few years we will be able to have real E-Masonry – virtual lodges where we can meet avatars and conduct ritual by means of a virtual reality structure."

Abundantly clear from the responses, 49%, is that E-Masonry in general and ML in particular offers an educational resource with which it is unlikely any single lodge or jurisdiction could compete. But we are very clear that is not primarily just because of the communication medium but rather that throughout its existence, ML has been blessed with members who are both Freemasons and scholars from different jurisdictions. One respondent wrote, *"Ideas flourish here. Answers to tough questions are always available. This could be a driving force behind revitalising Free-*

masonry." These people have patiently shared their knowledge and wisdom, provided a resource of learning and teaching and it is our great privilege to pay our tribute and heartfelt appreciation of their invaluable contribution. Below we will consider further the responses that have picked up on this theme.

Over 20% of the responses acknowledged that E-Masonry had broadened and diversified their understanding of Freemasonry. A respondent wrote, *"Any closed system will stagnate and eventually die without diversity. Diversity promotes evolution. At a basic level, E-Masonry enables masons to interact with thoughts and ideas outside of their closed system, local lodges and bring in new ideas, new energy promoting a diversity of thought, resulting in new experiences."*

For our own experience and that of the respondents we are clear that E-Masonry had provided something over and above that which the traditional practice of Freemasonry is providing. Answers to later questions will provide an indication of the impact, if any, that E-Masonry is making in the lodge and jurisdiction.

Q12 Do the Jurisdictions have policies on E-Masonic group membership.

Given that jurisdictions have policies on which lodges may or not be visited and the whole issue of "recognition", we wanted to know if members were aware of any policy pronouncement on e-Masonic group membership and what response the member might be making. Was it being perceived as a threat? If so how and why, and if not, why not, and might that be complacence?

A: Yes/No/Don't Know

Yes **16**
No **57**
Don't Know **14**

B: Anecdotal

"Don't really care; reading about what brothers in other parts of the world think and feel about our fraternity encourages me to reflect on what my views are."

"Some masons, lodges and obediences disapprove of virtual exchanges. My own WM tried to get me to leave one such list."

"None yet, but I can see it coming soon. I have some trepidation with this but am confident in the end the right decisions will be made."

"Admonishment re no chain letters or anything construed to precipitate a group protest or action."

"Don't ask" (2)

"Encourages it and supports more open masonry."

It would appear from the responses that there is not a concerted effort by jurisdictions to suppress cross-jurisdictional E-Masonry and that is most encouraging to learn. The view could perhaps be taken that jurisdictions may want to establish their own E-Masonry and that is something that we would welcome. Hopefully such a development would then not presage a prohibition on E-groups including non-recognised jurisdictions. It may be the case that Freemasons are already making "unauthorised" visits to non-recognised jurisdictions and as long as there is no precipitation it may not be a problem. We do not think that the ML group is a threat to jurisdictions or Freemasonry, but it may be a catalyst for change. Even if such change is valuable modernisation and future-proofing it may generate resistance; who better to shoot than the messenger?

The prohibition on visiting is perhaps something that is not given sufficient consideration. On the ML list it is unacceptable to refer to Freemasons from non-recognised jurisdictions as "clandestine" or "irregular". We are not aware of Freemasons being expelled because they have made unauthorised visits, if such happed it could well precipitate an international public relations disaster. If jurisdictions were to seek to prohibit membership of cross-jurisdictional E-groups there would be issues of enforcement. Also, there would the issue of how such a policy could be justified?

Unlike some of the respondents, we are optimistic that the positive roles of E-Masonry will be appreciated and this vital force will be harnessed to support a sustainable Freemasonry of the future.

Q13 Regular attendance at lodge.

There is a perception that lodge attendance is not as high as it might be and so we asked respondents if this is was due to the pressures of work, family or travel. For those with such pressures E-Masonry could be seen as a useful basis of support. However, with those three challenges covered, we were preparing for the possibility that E-Masonry might be an alternative to lodge attendance by some, on some occasions.

A: Yes/No

Yes **90**
No **12**

B: Anecdotal

"I travel to lodge every two months my membership of an E-group keeps me in touch."

It would seem that the question was blown away by the overwhelming majority of the sample. What can be claimed with certainty is that those who completed questionnaire regularly attend the lodge.

Q14 Are you active in the lodge

We were looking to see if E-Masons were active in their lodges and if any trends could be detected. For those that were not, we wanted to see if the responses gave any indication that E-Masonry activity might be, in any way, deterring participation in lodge activity.

Responses:

A: Yes/No

Yes **90***
No **19****

* Advised that they were lodge lecturers/educationalists **32**
** New Freemasons **6**

Again, the question was blown away. We did not invite respondents to provide details of their lodge activities but many were pleased to share them. That over a third are lodge lecturers/educationalists came as a welcome non-surprise.

The view is taken that if a person is serious about Masonic study, the preference for performing 1sts, 2nds or 3rds, or holding business meetings and lodges of instruction being lodges of rehearsal, does not allow for accessible resources or positive encouragement. Therefore lodge lecturers are self-produced! But, from where do they obtain their learning? Reading Masonic books perhaps? It cannot be, as one respondent has indicated, *"from the closed system of the lodge"*. We would suggest that it cannot be from any one jurisdiction either. Is it not the case that Freemasonry is divided over the globe into over two hundred different jurisdictions and they, in their own legitimacy and totality, are the reality of Freemasonry universal? But, unless the richness of this diversity is realised, and thereby informs research, then who are these lodge lecturers/educationalists and what are they talking about?

We know from our own experience and what the respondents have written that ML is a resource for Masonic learning and teaching. It is touching people and changing lives.

Therefore, what we can conclude with certainty is that the respondents to the questionnaire are active in their lodges. This can be understood as indicating that there would appear to be no evidence to suggest that those who are active on E-groups are not active in their lodges. But perhaps there are limits. Could there perhaps become a time when it may be necessary to choose between lodge activity and contributing to E-groups? If that did happen then upon what basis, and by using what criteria would decisions be made?

Q15 What are the challenges to traditional Freemasonry today and tomorrow

Obviously we wanted to know what were perceived to be the contemporary and possible future challenges to traditional Freemasonry to see if any of them might be being caused by E-Masonry. Also, there may be challenges, not caused by E-Masonry, but with it, in some existing or developed form, could be mitigated.

Responses:

A: Main Challenges

·	Recruitment and retention	38
·	Non-participation	16
·	Maintaining interest	16
·	Gaining new members of quality	14
·	Organisational overheads	13

- Lack of Lodge education   13
- Lack of attendance   8
- Inadequate Management/leadership   5
- Becoming irrelevant   5
- Growth too fast   4
- Negative publicity   3
- Work   3
- Resistance to change   3
- Anti-Masonic Pope
- Fragmentation of Freemasonry Universal
- The Orange Order.

The above list may contain but few surprises. It is not our intention to consider Freemasonry's challenges from within the traditional framework; our perspective is E-Masonry. Again, how much of the challenge is down to local leadership and how much is down from higher above? That only three respondents cited work as being a challenge is lower than anticipated especially as the majority of the respondents are of working age. Although we still believe those who have unpredictable work demands are less likely to be in Freemasonry and those considering petitioning a lodge would hesitate to do so until that situation changes, it still can be said that one makes time for what one truly wants or needs to do. However, should a person with a young family and a career to develop be spending significant or substantial amounts of time, mind or money on freemasonry or anything like it?

In Part 1, we briefly outlined the nature of the Masonic cultural phenomenon and its value basis. The view could be taken that there are more than enough people in the world with something like those values to maintain Masonic numbers. Given that a person shares the Masonic values, then E-Masonry could address challenges arising from maintaining interest and a lack of lodge and Masonic education. The above challenges could perhaps be regarded as "presenting" problems, that is to say, labels for more fundamental and significant problems. On respondents wrote, *"Loss of the meaning of masonry. In the 1700s it was a radical entity, today it is anything but."*

Contemporary Freemasonry is largely supportive of the incumbent liberal democracies tending, perhaps, a little to the right rather than the left. Perhaps the left right dichotomy is little more than a notional 5% difference in the tax take of the state and a debate over levels of bureaucracy. But, radical can be in either direction: what is Freemasonry's response to globalism, African poverty and the growing gap between rich and poor, global warming, the terrorist threat to name but a few items for next month's lodge business meeting? Perhaps the "people of quality" that Freemasonry once attracted would want to belong to organisations that are more connected to global issues and seeking radical responses. Or on the other hand, perhaps Freemasonry in the community is at a notional level and that Freemasonry as Freemasonry should seek to be demonstrably and explicitly at the heart and leading edge of local economies, community education, political systems and social organisations and not just be apologetically at the fringe. This would require a vision for which there does not seem to be heart and certainly no stomach to compete with political parties, religious organisations or the other diversions that occupy time, mind and money.

In our conclusions we will suggest how E-Masonry may be able arrest the impact of the identified challenges.

Q16 Should each GL/jurisdiction consider forming an E-group? Should each lodge consider forming an e-group?

A: Yes/No

GL/Jurisdiction
Yes **49**
No **33**

Lodge
Yes **29**

No **52**

We anticipated that more respondents would be support-ive of a jurisdictional E-group. It would be for those who did not want to be distracted by thinking from other jurisdictions or who did not want to risk the compromise of their oaths. A re-spondent wrote, *"It would never work for every lodge, but it should be something for each GL to consider."* We agree and would hope that every jurisdiction will give this consideration, undertake full consultation and come to a futuristic view.

On the other hand there were a significant number who wish to keep official Freemasonry and the e-group culture separate. *"No, I think E-groups should spring up spontaneously and develop their own characteristic "flavour".* And, *"No, ad hoc groups are best –most open, most responsive, most effective."*

It will be interesting to see if jurisdictions seek to develop E-Masonry. The case in terms of providing Masonic education and maintaining interest in the Craft may be substantial.

Q16 Even if there were to be official E-groups is there a role for other cross-jurisdictional E-groups.

Yes, we wanted to know if it was the case and if so, why?

A: Yes/No/Don't know

Yes	**105**
No	**0**
Don't Know	**1**

B: Reasons for Yes

Universal/ breadth/diversity	**78**
Freedom/free speech/freedom of thinking	3
Learning and substance	2
No mono-culture	1

To say that this is a substantial affirmation is an understatement! Perhaps this is a predictable response. The ML group is for Freemasons with an interest in cross jurisdictional communication and the 99% of respondents who represent 15% of the Group would be expected to choose this way.

Here is what they have said:

"Yes, the whole point is to learn how others do things."

"Yes, we are free to do as we wish."

"Yes, I would definitely belong to other groups. I want to experience the variety of positions held by my brothers and sisters regardless of jurisdiction. And, I want to truly dream of a way to find common ground among all jurisdictions."

"Variety is the spice of life and Freemasonry needs all the spice it can get."

"Yes, each E-group has its own purpose."

"Each group maintains its own personality and these different viewpoints, while not always in agreement with mine, are fundamental to universalism and tolerance."

"I probably would to maintain contact with certain people I've met."

"The GL is very controlling, monitors everything and has actually shut down a chat room on us. So, we try to talk about masonry without constriction and big brothers."

We can but hope that jurisdictions will respect the views of this, albeit but small, sample and not seek to proscribe its communications. We believe most mainstream Freemasons are largely unaware of Co-Masonry and other unrecognized Masonic jurisdictions, let alone concerned about how relationships between all global Freemasonic jurisdictions could impact the future of the Craft for years to come.

Q17 The Masonic Light group welcomes Freemasons from all world-wide Masonic jurisdictions. Please describe how, if at all, this has affected your view of the Craft from a global perspective.

We believed it to be the case that most Freemasons rarely have communications outside of their jurisdictions. The universality of E-Masonry in general and ML in particular has brought together Freemasons who, via traditional communication, would never have met. It has brought together communication among Freemasons whose jurisdictions would not recognise that some of them are Freemasons at all! We wanted to know what impression, if any, this had made on the members. Therefore, for this question, there is no counting, it is just an expression of how people are feeling.

> *"With 50+ years as a mason I have discovered things about the craft that I never dreamed existed."*

> *"It has made me more excited than ever* (23 years in Craft) *about being a mason. I enjoy the diverse opinions and it helps _me_ decide which foreign jurisdictions I should visit."*

> *"It was a wonderful discovery of how I can call Masons world-wide, true brothers and sisters"*

> *"Helped me to re-think my position on Freemasonry, freemasons and most of all about myself, my Masonic engagement and my life engagements in general."*

"I am much more open to a wider view of the Craft in all its varieties than I would have been without E-Masonry."

"It confirms my belief that humanity is collectively evolving in spiritual consciousness and that Masonry as a vehicle of that evolution represents the kids at the head of the class. Not indicative of everyone, of course, but certainly an incubator for world leadership."

We regard the above responses as a serious vindication of E-Masonic activity. It is clear from the whole of these responses, and many others, that the traditional jurisdictional primacy has been challenged. It is perhaps the case that there is more to Freemasonry than "my" jurisdiction and those which it wants to choose to recognize. That is to say, *I* want to choose the jurisdictions that I will recognise. *I* want to choose the lodges that I would like to visit. Whether it is a lodge under the Grand Lodge of France, American Federation of Human Rights, the Greek Federation of Le Droit Humain, or the Prince Hall Grand Lodge of Alabama, *I* want to decide where my Freemasonry takes me.

On the other hand, there are some respondents whose position is perhaps somewhat yet to be determined!

"Although still strongly against co-masonic lodges, I enjoy the discussion on this topic and am still learning."

"I do not like the clandestine types of masonry. I do however like to hear from regular brothers from around the world."

"Its reinforced my perceptions that there are all kinds of ways to be a mason but even if some of them are foreign and even anathema to me, that doesn't render them irrelevant to everybody. It reinforces the Masonic notion of tolerance."

"With ML I tend to be less active because some of the members are from clandestine Masonic bodies."

"…….because of the diversity of the membership, various jurisdictions and the impression they have made upon me and the way
I feel about the Craft."

"……the basic tenets of Freemasonry are world-wide."

"The whole point is to learn how others do things."

"We are one fraternity facing the same issues and problems."

"It has made me realise that that there are may in mainstream
masonry that see the importance of recognising mixed or female
masonry which is a heartening thing to see."

"The diversity is very enriching and enlightening."
"It has made me more tolerant of others, their ideas and thoughts."

"It has shown me how parochial and close-minded the Craft can
be and yet how much hope there is."

"It has simply given me a better understanding of the fraternity."

"I am more accepting of other Masonic views, despite the opposi-
tion of my GL."

"It's a ray of hope, that the profane and the ruffians are not all the
temples yet."

"Although UGLE is the oldest, that does not make it the only
"right" way to do things."

"It is fascinating to be able to se how other masons operate, and all
from my desk."

"Has provided the opportunity to become a well-rounded mason."

"Brilliant; mainstream masons are made aware that there are other legitimate Masonic orders out there."

"I do not think that Freemasonry should be called universal, in fact it is clannish."

"Masonry is adjusted by jurisdictions, but it doesn't belong to them. I feel Masonic enough in random Masonic environments, which has nothing to do with the tyled lodges that I attend."

"We are told that masonry is spread over the four divisions of the globe, but you can't appreciate that sitting in rubber-boot-township."

"I'm a bit leary on sharing communication with clandestine Masons."

"Because of the diversity o f its members, the ML Group encourages free discussion, my Masonic world has become a much larger place and makes me realise that it is a privilege to be a mason even if not recognised by all."

"We are all ultimately from the one family of beliefs."

" It has caused me to be observant of the fact that there are people around the world who refer to themselves as masons though I don't recognise them as such."

"I can see vast changes in men's attitudes. It's nice to get pats on the electronic back from them instead of rocks."

"My eyes have been opened, and patience and tolerance and compassion have been developed in my life."

"It has made me less likely to react with cynicism or paranoia about unrecognised groups."

"Opened my eyes to many options for me in my Masonic journey."

"We need to break down artificially constructed walls."

"It has reinforced the universal nature of the Craft and given me new insights into other ways of doing the same thing."

"It has tended to breakdown strict ideas of regularity and recognition. I think these will have to be changed in the long run. It may also provide the core of active Masons who will help bring this about. My own view of things has been broadened."

"None...my obligations are my obligations."

"Puts one's own jurisdiction in its place; one, and not superior, among many."

"Seeing the diversity and yet rejoicing in the things we have in common."

Q18 Any comments on E-Masonry and its possible development.

An open-ended question; a final trawl to obtain any additional thoughts on E-Masonry not captured by earlier questions.

A: Masonic Light in particular

It was most encouraging that nearly 50% respondents expressed sincere gratitude for the benefits they had received from ML communications. It must be doing something right for some Freemasons and that assurance will provide the energy to continue operations. *"I can't think of a thing you haven't done already. Thank you Josh, I wonder how many masons and lodges have ben-*

efited from ML? You my Brother have made a positive impact on ma-
sonry in general probably more than you ever intended." **(30)**

We were grateful to those who made suggestions for, in their view, the even more effective operation of ML.

Stricter moderation	**3**
Cross the line three times then out.	**3**
Needs sub-moderators to help out.	
Limit to four E-mails per person per thread.	

It is the case, as clearly indicated in responses to earlier questions, that some postings have caused offence: E-Masonry is in its infancy. It has yet to survive growing pains and grow up. We still take the view that peer moderation is by far the most appropriate form of ensuring that the inappropriateness of any postings will be brought to the attention of those responsible. Matters of E-communication style also have yet to evolve, gain consensus and bed down. On the ML group the only thing that will not be tolerated is intolerance itself. The raison d'etre of the group is a recognition and celebration of Freemasonry universal in all its forms and has been clearly expressed since the beginning that being different doesn't mean being wrong! The Moderator is committed to the continuous improvement of the ML group and will continue to work with members to ensure that process is achieved with all its wonderful potential outcomes.

B: E-Masonry in general

"I think that you need to define what E-Masonry is. Is it discussion forums or an attempt at a tyled lodge on-line?"

"E-Masonry is a wonderful thing; I just hope that we never try to replace the lodge experience on-line."

Whilst we do not claim to have coined the term "E-Masonry", we are not aware of seeing it written before we started on this book. But as we believe that this is a first published attempt to understand the phenomenon then yes, a definition should indeed be considered. Already we have suggested that the phenomenon of Freemasonry can be understood in its particular ethical take on the cultural areas of work, education, citizenship, religiosity, fraternity, charity and gender. E-Masonry is a possible means of, in a changing world, ensuring that those values can be supported in a medium suited to futurity.

Therefore, our suggested definition: "E-Masonry is an additional, online, way of achieving daily Masonic advancement." As indicated in responses to earlier questions, members of ML are overwhelmingly regular attendees at lodge meetings and are active in masonry, so are we. It has not entered our heads that E-Masonry could or should replace the traditional practice of Freemasonry, it will add to it but in so doing it will bring about changes. These changes can be justified if they make the practice of Freemasonry more consonant with contemporary and future lifestyles.

"Maybe one day technology will allow video interaction to be as common as e-mail."

"E-Masonry could become a central archive for all Masonic research."

"At times I have been disheartened by the deriding of co-masonry but generally the environment is enlightened and supportive. Any e-mail list that promotes greater tolerance in the Masonic community is of immeasurable value."

"Perhaps obtain support from mason in each country and get some "local" social events going."

"Better use of files and photo album."

"Less bla bla, more symbolism and personal work, less café/bar discussions and NO shouts."

"Superficiality will take the life out of E-Masonry as well."

"Should rebut the charges made by traditionalists preaching about the evils of masonry in the chat rooms."

"Attach thumbnail image with each post."

"Discourteous postings will cause GLs to seek our closure."

"Steps towards mobile lodges. Work makes many of us mobiles."
"Should formulate rules for composing and responding posts."

"Improve files and links."

"Should be designed to broaden knowledge of the Craft. Local lodges will become less important over time. Will be a balancing act, lodge v E-Masonry, this is a new paradigm for future masons."

"Develop vocal communications."

Interesting to see if E-Masonry takes on a life of its own. Would be really good if it could be seen as supportive of Freemasonry universally.

"I'm in the Group for the selfish reason of wanting to learn. I hope I am able to give something back."

"ML could become the VR server for the virtual lodge, quite literally opening the path."

Summary:

As indicated, we are so grateful to those of the ML membership who troubled to respond to the questionnaire. We are astonished at many of the responses and the comments made. We would not wish to extrapolate from this sample, of just over one hundred, more than what may be justified. But we will intriguingly ponder just how many more "regular" freemasons may be like-minded or could become so given exposure to seriously universal, cross-jurisdictional freemasonry, courtesy of E-communication.

In Part I we suggested in broad overview the nature of the Masonic phenomenon and how it may be being stalked by the E-revolution. In Part Two we shared the experience of the ML group from the perspective of its founder-Moderator. With the benefit of the questionnaire responses, we have shared the experience of over a hundred members – the highs and lows; the face of our E-masonry, warts and all. Again we do thank the respondents for their considered replies. In the final part we will be giving expression to what some may perceive to be a novel idea, that of freemasonry being openly at the centre of the community and democratically providing its leadership. Perhaps not novel but a return to where we were.

Chapter 4:

The confluence of two cultures

Our exploratory essay opened with an initial examination of the phenomena of traditional Freemasonry and that of the recently arrived E-masonry. The nature of traditional Freemasonry was considered in terms of how it has been manifested in the seven cultural characteristics of:- the work ethic, education, citizenship, religiosity, fraternity, charity and gender. How E-communication may have impacted in these areas was also briefly considered. We have undertaken a survey among E-masons and now, as enlightened by their responses, we wish to reconsider the two phenomena of traditional Freemasonry and E-masonry. The purpose is to see if the responses have provided any insight into the possibility that E-masonry may be able to complement traditional Masonic practice, supplement any inadequacies that there might be, and thereby assist with the sustainability of Masonic values, in some due form, into the future.

As previously indicated, the responses contained views that were somewhat other than we had anticipated. This required us to think more extensively and radically than we had expected. We had underestimated the impact that over six years of cross-jurisdictional E-masonry had made on the members of the list and that very much included ourselves. Perhaps it was not so much a wake-up call as rather it was a milestone in our experience: certainly it was a time for pause and reflection. Again, we had become so accustomed to the breadth and depth of the Masonic education that was available through the list that, in common with many respondents, we began to wonder how we would have known anything had it not been for Masonic E-communication.

With the other members, we believed that we had come to know and create an affinity with people that we had not seen. This seemed to favourably compare, in whole or in part, with the affinity that existed between lodge members who had been "known" for some time.

The respondents made it overwhelmingly clear that they wanted cross-jurisdictional communication even if E-masonry was officially made available via jurisdiction or lodge. This seemed to us to contain an explicit challenge to the traditional jurisdictional prerogatives around recognition and visitation; implicitly, this was indicating a challenge to the concepts of "mainstream", "regular" and "clandestine". Meeting-up was beginning to happen, and where it wasn't, there was a clear aspiration for this to occur. There was an emerging practice for members, intending to travel anywhere in the world, to share this with the group and at the speed of light, responses assuring of warm welcomes were being received from lodges and Freemasons in the locality.

When lodge attendance was not possible or in-between attendances, E-masonry was proving to be a means of support and a resource for the maintenance of interest in the Craft. Many comments were made indicating that, for a variety of reasons, E-masonry was not only sustaining, but was proving to be a sustainable form of Masonic experience. It can be fitted between other commitments; it is available 24 hours per day, 7 days per week and 365 days per year. It saved the need to travel; it was cost effective and stimulating, calming and consoling. It was becoming for some, if not a way of life, then certainly a valued part of their daily routine and we would respectfully suggest a significant part of their Masonic improvement.

It is with thoughts such as this that we turn to the seven aspects of culture, the mark that E-communications may have made and to where it might lead.

The work ethic:

We did not make specific enquiries in the questionnaire pertaining to matters of work and the work-place; therefore, this did not feature at all strongly among the responses even though the majority were from people of recognisably working age. For the most of the sample there did not seem to be inordinate work pressures. We do not know if this really is the case or if work pressures were understated - we didn't ask specific or penetrative questions. Traditionally, Freemasons have been drawn from the professions, business, proprietorships and officers both civil and military. Essentially they were of the backbone of local economies and meetings provided the opportunity to mull over matters of local trade and government. The Diary of Samuel Pepys provides an insight, *"And thence to Trinity House, being invited to an Elder Brother's feast. And there sat by Mr. Prin and he had good discourse about the privileges of Parliament ..."* We are not suggesting for a moment that S. Pepys Esq. was a Freemason or that the occasion was Masonic, but we are persuaded that it was from within this milieu that Speculative Freemasonry took its rise.

Lodge attendance was a part of how business was undertaken – indeed, oiling the wheels of local industry. Therefore as lodge attendance was, in part, one of the ways in which business was conducted, it would not be an imposition to plan work around lodge hours and to invite key colleagues and associates to petition for initiation. There was less mobility, movement of staff and shorter travel to work distances. It may be the case that there are now more in Freemasonry who are drawn from among self-employed tradesmen and employees. But Freemasons do not now meet and mull over matters of local trade and politics and are not seeking to inform local decisions - complain about them, maybe yes. (It perhaps would be an interesting line of enquiry to find out just what Freemasons do talk about when at something like a festive board.)

It would appear to be the case that locally grown businesses are no longer at the heart of local economies this may mean that Freemasons are no longer there either. At the heart of local economies are branches of corporations led by seriously mobile and younger managers engaged in business plans, profit margins, book to bill ratios, strategic supply and volatile staff dynamics. Their hours are longer and unpredictable; they often do not have significant local connections or engagement and many of them are female! The arrangement of the male being the single-handed bread winner with the female in domestic support and motherhood has largely been superseded by a lifestyle partnership dependent on two salaries. There is a diminution of a gender stereotyped demarcation of responsibilities and there is wider male participation and domesticity; indeed, it may well be the case that the male of the species has become house trained. This would militate against a young male professional from having significant regular social commitments at all and certainly those of a type that would exclude his partner from membership. Given that meetings of Freemasons are no longer meetings of the leadership of the local economy, there is no longer a business case or justification for attending the lodge or undertaking Masonic commitments.

Computer systems, as management tools, are enabling substantially greater control. Instant communications mean that management and employees cannot hide; their performance is under continuous review and there is little in the way of downtime. In the last two decades, people who would have been considered Masonic material live in households that contain an office often with the technology to access corporate systems from home. Also, contact with "corporate" can be made from the remotest locations.

In theory, this could give rise to more flexible working such as hot-desking, touch-down centres and more working from home, but these possibilities do not appear to be gathering any real significant momentum. Given globalisation and corporate identity, much of contemporary working is process orientated, work-station based and controlled. Most employees have a place in the process that does not require or accommodate much by way of creativity and prima donnas are not suffered lightly. Indeed, the contemporary emphasis on team working is reducing the role of individuality and replacing it with a reinforced corporate identity. The continuous change and up-grading of E-systems, that E-working is generating, means that much more time has to be devoted in keeping up to date. Swings in markets, products and the availability of labour are more volatile, regulation more intrusive and therefore survival and success is dependent on training and re-training - management and employee engaged in life-long learning.

As it must be concluded that lodges are no longer at the centre of local business affairs in a way that perhaps resembled a former role, the question arises as how the contemporary work ethic is manifested in the lodge? It must be the case that within a lodge there would be an expectation that a Freemason would be a valued employee? Today, it might well be indisputable that, retention in a job is proof enough of a person's ability and assiduity. If a Freemason is repeatedly fired from jobs there is perhaps less of a basis for self-respect and a lessening of esteem from fellow masons. That is to say, success in ones work-life remains the most fundamental and primary test of Masonic merit; indeed, the manifestation of the work ethic.

However, the view can be taken that learning and performing ritual is a most important demonstration of the worthiness of Freemason. A good ritualist demonstrates work well accomplished and a serious commitment to Freemasonry. Usually, such a Freemason would be a highly valued member of a lodge. In many jurisdictions, this may be the main basis for promotion and Masonic honours. If a person shows no interest in the ritual, their commitment to Freemasonry may be unclear; if a person is unwilling to "progress", it is a challenge to the lodge management – it may not be effective! It is accepted as being one of the merits of Freemasonry that people who are unaccustomed to being in leadership positions or in prominent roles can, through increased practice of the ritual, become more competent, confident and assertive. But many organisations can provide a similar basis for such self-development. When more of Freemasonry's numbers were from the local leadership elite, learning and performing ritual was perhaps easier, especially as in the past there would have been more resonance with the language and its implicit religiosity.

There are websites from which the words of the ritual and perambulations can be learned. This could minimise the need to travel to lodges of rehearsal and allow Freemasons to learn in their own time and at their own convenience. It is clear that when ritual is being performed there is often very little engagement with any meaning the words may have had, or have, and it is clear from the questionnaire responses that lodges have little time for any "learning" other than practicing ritual. It may well be the case that this type of "working" in the lodges is in decline as so much time is absorbed up by holding down a job and business travel. This may not allow too much time or mind for learning ritual, deciding on its moral imperative and its practical outworking – other than, as in being a good employee, picking up the domestic financial commitment and having time and resource to enjoy leisure and convivial socialising. What, though, about a daily advancement in Masonic knowledge and in making the liberal arts and sciences a daily study?

The value of education:

It is clear from the responses that the majority of the members of the ML group are there to learn about Freemasonry, its origins, meaning and significance in their daily life. They have told us that their lodges do not provide this and there is little appetite for the lodges so to do. Capacity is absorbed with other business. Just as in the contemporary successful work-place, lifelong learning is a requirement, so to in the life of a Freemason. There is a requirement for daily advancement in matters Masonic - improvement. Or put another way, daily progress is achieved by in making a person a better person, but on what is such progress based? It is unlikely to study of "the" VSL that is to say Volume of Sacred Law – a generic term for the recognized Holy Book of a Freemason's particular religion or more pragmatically, a text that will reinforce the taking of an oath. But, might it be based on other forms of learning? In any worthy form of life there is no standing still. E-communication has made great strides possible in distance learning and course members are tutored in E-groups. Distance learning has enabled serious study to be undertaken whilst working. This thereby provides and creates the convenience to accommodate study and an ability to meet its cost in time and price.

The ability of the Masonic Light group to be able to provide and support education for Freemasons can be attributed to the very good fortune of there being, within the group, handfuls of members who were, and are, able and apt to teach. The rest of us have, electronically, sat at their feet. The Moderator has from time to time introduced features to provide some semblance of programmed learning. But, most of the teaching and learning has been in quantum randomness; although, none the less valuable for that. The usefulness of the discussion that has been generated by current affairs and its significance for Freemasons can not be over-stated as evidenced by the survey responses. It has enabled and facilitated a connection with Freemasonry and what is going on in the world. It has replaced the isolation of irrelevance; how can we begin to measure the learning impact of 75,000+ E-mails? That ML members have been able to discuss, by and large, without implosion, many seriously emotive matters is a great credit to the group and augurs favourably for the future of the medium. It is clear that teaching on ML has come from men and women who have a total commitment to lifelong learning and who have areas of expertise that is from both within, and from outside of , their day jobs. Also, it is clear from ML communications that there is much more for Freemasons to learn than just the origins of Freemasonry, the transmutation from operative to "speculative" or the split and union of the Antients and the Moderns. Indeed, so very much more.

Apart from occasional lectures of dubious value, it is the case that lodges are not committed to providing useful learning programmes. The jurisdictions could produce learning programmes for new Freemasons, material that is preparatory for becoming a Freemason and even "advanced" education materials for Master Masons who are seeking further light and deeper meaning within the teachings of the Craft. To some extent, E-masonry could be the first steps on this Masonic pathway. It could appeal to younger and busier people with family commitments who are still making their financial way. It opens up new opportunities for time management and could provide that most desirable of commodities – flexibility. Yet, the opportunities can still remain for learning and socialising in convivial company.

Perhaps it is the case that Freemasons should be characterised by a commitment to lifelong learning, building upon education already received and developing it further. The world of learning has never been more accessible. Masonic E-groups do offer tremendous scope for learning but they are no substitute for academic based learning. What we are saying is that Freemasons should go back to "school", remain in study mode and share what they are learning with other Freemasons. E-groups would be one way for that to be achieved. We believe that "studious" should be a defining characteristic among Freemasons. In addition to teaching within lodges and Masonic networks, Freemasons should be a source of learning and education to and within their communities. But, is knowledge power? Are the people committed to life-long learning the ones who might, or should be, operating the levers of power at the heart of the political process? Who better for such a leadership role than free and accepted masons?

Participatory citizenship:

Those who are creating wealth and who are committed to lifelong learning may well wish to inform the decision-making process. (Perhaps they have a duty to do so!) This could be achieved by voting in elections, standing for office, joining pressure groups or by being in spheres of influence. Freemasons, just like anyone else, and notwithstanding strange loyal oaths, are permitted to overthrow governments, as long as they do it by constitutional means. However, if governments choose to attack Freemasonry or its values, then as previously indicated, it is not unlikely that Freemasons, in or out of Freemasonry, will occupy in various forms of resistance.

Voting in elections was once a minority privilege; sufferance has become increasingly universal, yet the percentage of voters exercising this right, in the older "democracies", would seem to be in decline. There seems to be some significant measure of disengagement between leaders and those being led. In many cases the perceived choice between parties and candidates may be insufficient to create a level of interest that would risk overloading the vote count system. It is likely that for most Freemasons the choice would be for a lesser extent of government and the presumed corollary of a reduced tax take.

It may well be the case that the world's political topography is changing. The rise of "Speculative" Freemasonry may well have coincided with the rise of the nation state. Perhaps two World Wars have challenged the concept of the nation state and there is increased consideration of one world or globalism; although, the possibility that these terms may not interchange and may have different meanings for different people is not lost on us. Perhaps other than the G8 group of countries, any concept of any political mechanisms that may be underpinning a global economy is definitely lost on us. But, we would require a seriously rigorous conspiracy theory for us to begin to believe that there may be a G8 lodge over and above jurisdictions and uniting, the two hundred or so of them that currently exist, in some sort of global conspiracy! But of course, if we did know of one, would we talk about it?

Seemingly, politics is being conducted at stratospherical level. And, if that is the case, the view can be taken that this could lead to a groundswell that might address a political vacuum at the street corner. There may be an emergence of some green shoots of a localism, not necessarily based upon traditional political parties, that is springing up to reinforce the concept and reality of community. Travelling miles and miles for work and to lodges may seem heroic, but is it sustainable? How can a Freemason be effective in his or her own community if they are never in it, or part of it? We are prepared to go as far as to suggest that a Freemasonry that is not shining as a wealth creator, educator or political leader in a community may be a Freemasonry that is of no relevance at all. Wealth is not confined to finance. A community's wealth can be advanced when its citizens are active participants in enhancing the well-being of all: from shovelling the snow from an elderly couple's sidewalk to organizing a game of soccer for the children in the neighbourhood. Freemasons ought to be leaders, mentors and dare we suggest "role models". That is to imply, faith without works is dead.

Surely Freemasons, those who are successful in work and apt to teach must have something to offer their communities - something like leadership! If they haven't, it must raise serious questions about the self and mutual value of Freemasonry in general and of Freemasons in particular. Communities are dynamic organisms in various states of development, but it is not always easy to define their spatial limits; but, that of course is no reason for declining to make a start. Political boundaries may be a start but they might not necessary encompass a social reality and therefore are not the only guide to the delineation of a community. There may already be a party political structure in place but as indicated above, there may not necessarily be anything like a meaningful engagement with the process by the citizens.

110

This leaves open the possibility for citizens to challenge institutions and take more control of their own lives. The faceless bureaucrat from the state capital cannot possibly know enough to know what will enhance the quality of life in the hugely various communities that make up a diverse nation. This bureaucrat cannot often imagine, let alone sustain, the improvements that can change lives for the better. It is only when a problem is addressed locally, on a human scale, by human beings who can see what is happening to other human beings that people and their well-being can make progress. If political economy is at a stratospherical level then sustainability will require a connection and engagement at the street corner.

There are three issues that impact upon communities and around which all Freemasons can unite. They are:- the expansion of the local economy, an increase in social justice and an increasingly inspiring environment. These things can only be promoted with a partnership of business, knowledge and care – Freemasons must be in there somewhere! If that means less ritual and less lodge business then fine, if lodge activities are not touching the community through the actions of its members, then are they much more than an eccentric indulgence? Worse, is it just an escape? And, worst of all, is it an irrelevance?

Earlier we have suggested that Freemasonry is not a spectator sport; we further suggest that a worthy life isn't either. Surely a serious essence of Freemasonry is participation as it is through which that Masonic commitment and learning can be demonstrated. In some jurisdictions, there is contained within the ritual a commitment for freemasons to be the better enabled to be of service to mankind. Surely that is more than charitable giving. It may be ambitious to suggest that the lodge could become the centre of a community but a centre for the community yes or perhaps, think the unthinkable, close the lodge building down and meet in and with the community.

Just image if the Freemasons of a community were united and had candidates standing in local elections! Their manifesto could be based upon the Declaration of Human Rights; the localisation of the seven cultural features introduced in this text and summarised in the three principles of, growing local economies, increased social justice and an enhancement of environmental quality. Imagine if the energy that is being poured into Masonic activity, combined with the organisational and planning facility, enabled by E-communication, was focused on winning seats in local elections. Given that Freemasons should be the epitome of trustworthiness and sound judgement, then surely these men and women could turn the world, not upside down, but perhaps the right way up!

It is perhaps undeniable that the rise of globalism, as is, has been enabled and facilitated by E-communication and that it will depend on even more enhanced E-sophistication as it seeks to map the world in terms of commodities and markets. Communication is key to most successful undertakings and that would also apply at the community level. So also is organisation as an activity, but as soon as the shift is made from verb to noun and becomes "the" organisation, focus is often lost. Organisations tend to take on a life of their own and their agendas supersede the purposes and people for whom they were originally intended. What becomes primal is the survival of "the organisation" for its own sake – even if it has lost its way and even if it has failed to adapt to a changing environment. E-groups of various types seem to be binding people together. Suppose that each community was united in an E-group through which all decisions affecting the community could be discussed and voted upon. Imagine that all Freemasons in a community, regardless of jurisdiction, provided open and worthy participation and leadership as Freemasons! Such is not the Utopianism that perhaps enthused early "speculative" Freemasons, but it may well lead to a better land.

Unless Freemasonry's values are challenged by the state, there is no need for secrecy and pretences of it are a liability. What sort of man would join Freemasonry believing that they could learn something of any worth that could not be Googled! Therefore we are looking beyond openness, we are looking at integration! If Freemasonry is not a secret ruling elite, then let us stop the aloofness and separation and become a part of the community. Perhaps, it is only when there is a clash between the values of the state and those of Freemasonry that the reality of the Masonic vision can be tested. This clash could only be over the role and rights of the individual and, as was tested in the UK in the late 1990s, would likely to be contrary to The Declaration of Human Rights. If Freemasonry was an inextricable part of community reality, it would take incredible brutality to implement its repression. It would, as before, go underground and likely as before, re-emerge to demonstrate its irrepressibility. In some jurisdictions, Masonic oaths are taken on a copy of The Declaration of Human Rights. Given that the core Masonic values are enshrined in the Declaration, is it perhaps too much, even to conceive, that a day might come when all Freemasons, of all jurisdictions, would unite in this way. For this to be possible it will be necessary for Freemasonry to have to come to terms with the religiosity that has thus far be-devilled it for much too long.

The bind of religiosity:

It is clear from ML postings that the members of the group have diverse perspectives on matters of religion and spirituality. They vary from a belief that their monotheistic religions and Freemasonry are indivisible, through deism, pantheism and natural religion to that of self-professed atheism. As the questionnaire responses have shown, without the benefit of something like E-masonry, there is no concept of the diversity that is out there - both within and between jurisdictions. Yet we co-exist. We are persuaded that it is appropriate for Freemasonry to provide a spiritual component for those who want it. Some, of course might not, those who choose to describe experience in exclusively empirical terms. It has to be accepted that for some, describing experience in terms of spirituality may not require the vocabulary of a recognisable faith system or membership of a denominated faith community. Also, and vitally for them, their spirituality might not require concepts that extend beyond space and time. We are persuaded, from over 75,000 E-mails that the consideration of a spirituality that may not extend beyond space and time is not a place to which every enquirer may have chosen to journey.

Some Freemasons do not accept that this life is but a preparation for another, but that does not mean that they can not be "Freemasons". One of the problems with the "preparation" view is that it reduces goodness to an individual and selfish expedient. That is to say, it leaves no distinction between good works and paying premiums for fire insurance. Surely the ethical basis of Freemasonry is respect for the rest of the members of humankind, a celebration of strengths, developing potential and supporting people in times of genuine need. We are at a loss to understand how some jurisdictions can require not just a belief in a supreme being but a belief in the immortality of the soul and in the resurrection of the dead. The view has to be taken that in many cases, Speculative Freemasonry has been assimilated within the monotheistic religions of a given geographic region and that Masonic values have been subsumed into religious ones. Perhaps it is time for Freemasonry to come out of the cloisters!

It is likely to be the case that Speculative Freemasonry took its rise from a time when non-conformity with the state recognised religion was viewed with suspicion and perceived as being a threat. The genius of the first published "speculative" Masonic constitution was that on matters of religion, it was short, ambiguous and obscure with vague notions of "supreme beings" and "divine architects" replacing specific dogma. Indeed, where does theology end and casuistry begin? It is not clear, with what balance of theology and casuistry, that Masonic jurisdictions approached the relationship of religion and the Craft. Perhaps it really is the case that in "speculative" Freemasonry, the person of God has been replaced by the concept of God. That is to say, to be an accepted Freemason is possible providing that there is some verbal acceptance of something outside and beyond the self. An atheist is one who believes that the world revolves around themselves, the culture of "me, I and myself". Such people are not fit to be Freemasons unless they are joining in order to be assisted to change such an unsustainable world-view. We are suggesting that if a supreme being is defined as being a personal deity, impersonal deity, cosmic intelligence or even Mother Nature, then perhaps the term "atheist" fails to inform anybody about anything that is useful. Freemasonry recognises that the good of the individual can only be pursued in the context of the wider good. But, you do not have to be religious to be unselfish.

Freemasonry will, very wisely, not want to know anything of the details of this "supreme being" other than that a person believes in he and/or she and/or it. This however leaves open the possibility that it could be "God" as understood by one of the monotheistic religions or a "supreme being" of ones own creation. This may well be of concern to the leaderships and apologists of the revealed religions because, as it is not permitted to discuss in the lodge the nature of an individual supreme being, the concept may be at serious variance with a revealed mono-God. Some regard not discussing in the lodge one's concept of "supreme being" as being of great wisdom, others may regard it at best as obfuscation and in the worst case, dishonesty. What is agreed is that "speculative" Freemasonry, with its pan-supreme beings, could not survive if these things were discussed!

We didn't need the spelling and grammar checker to advise that the term "supreme being" should normally have the benefit of capitals "S" and "B". (Perhaps Freemasons have infiltrated the Microsoft Corporation.) We suggest that the spelling and grammar checker should also be troubled by the question, "Do you believe in a Supreme Being?" Surely there cannot be <u>a</u> Supreme Being, only <u>The</u> Supreme Being or can there be polytheism of Supreme Beings? If the question was posed as, do you believe in the <u>concept</u> of The/a S/supreme B/being, as something outside and beyond us, everyone could, in some way, sign up in acceptation. For some however, the concept of "supreme being" may be outside and beyond but may be confined within the limits of space and time. But, nobody would know, because these things are not discussed in the lodge. Therefore you could answer yes to a belief in the/a S/supreme B/being and be an atheist as traditionally defined. In light of this, it is suggested that the question may serve no useful purpose whatsoever!

Again, as in many jurisdictions, the question of a belief in a supreme being is asked verbally and this therefore leaves open the possibility for "being" to be understood as a verb. If that can be permitted, then to believe in supreme being may surely be something to which everyone could concur and in which case, again, the question means nothing, achieves a false impression and provides no basis for a meaningful unity. The reason for a belief in a supreme being may be based on no more than a belief that atheists, by definition were not, and still cannot be, trustworthy persons and that you can not believe what they say because they won't take an oath on a VSL. If that is the case, such a reason is hardly appropriate for the Twenty First century. What authority can there be for asking such a question or what Masonic purpose is achieved by a meaningless affirmation to such a vague notion?

We struggle with a proposition on the lines of Freemasonry being neither a religion nor a substitute for religion. A person can make whatever they want to be their religion: an organisation that is a peculiar system of morality, veiled in allegory and illustrated by symbols may well be the apotheosis of a religion! It is accepted that the leadership of a jurisdiction may have some ownership of the term "Freemasonry" and how it may be defined; but, the language does have a life of its own. Therefore, we respectfully suggest that no jurisdiction has the prerogative to define "religion". A suggestion that Freemasonry may not be a substitute for religion is interesting. That may well be the case but it also must be conceded that for many Freemasons it is, in practice, an alternative world-view to that proposed by religions. We have suggested that Freemasonry is a template to make sense

116

of this life for its own sake and not for the sake of another life on some different basis outside and beyond the paradigm of space and time. In light of this we do struggle with why some jurisdictions require a belief in the immortality of the soul and the resurrection of the body even after cremation.

We believe that Freemasonry should be open to any person who wishes to improve themselves for the purpose of being of more service to humankind. This of course may include people who belong to a faith system but maybe not. However, we return to a view expressed earlier pertaining to members of revealed religions wishing to become Freemasons. The issue is, why would the member of a revealed religion want to become a Freemason? What is it that Freemasonry can offer that the religion cannot? Is Freemasonry making up for a perceived, but not articulated, inadequacy in that religion? It is accepted that for, any number of reasons, people may wish to preserve the outer appearances of religious conformity even though there is no personal engagement with it, or commitment, or reality. It does seem to be the case that some people are without religious convictions yet seek an outward conformity; we regard this as habit of religiosity and accept that it has been pan-endemic for some time. Perhaps some people are not clear where conviction ends and appearances begin.

That is fine as long as the religious people joining Freemasonry accept that they are, joining with people who may not be of similar religious persuasion, do not feel unequally yoked to them, and do not have a proselytising compulsion towards them. The ritual may well appeal to them as it is based upon the Old Testament, a text that finds a consensus of acceptation by the three leading revealed monotheistic religions. But, what may appear to be an inconsistency is the fact that Masonic proceedings appear to have what are indistinguishable from, hymns, prayers and allusions to a shared deity. We have already demonstrated that no such shared deity can be assumed! To allow that Freemasons are all singing away to a different deity is surely very odd.

We can see no problem with having the ritual based upon Old Testament portions providing that they can be understood as being allegorical; that is to say, words from which moral and ethical lessons may be extracted. However, and thinking of the future, there is increasingly less popular resonance with the O.T. and the concept of there being a volume of sacred law fixed for time and eternity is becoming less convincing. Attendance at religious services is in substantial decline and that is something from which the leaders of Masonic constitutions could usefully learn. Religions are turning to websites, E-groups and house-groups. The maintenance of religious buildings of historical or architectural significance may not constitute the principle ministry of the disciples of a deity. It may detract resources of time, mind and money from better things; it may be a materialistic distraction from a spiritual calling – church buildings are being sold daily. Similarly, Freemasons may have better things to do than to maintain buildings. The building of King Solomon's Temple is allegorical and perhaps it can be achieved without a local Masonic temple or a grand jurisdiction headquarters. That is not to say we should necessarily meet outside in a local park, that we do not appreciate fine architecture or we are not grateful for the edifices passed on to us from previous generations. It is however becoming a reality that the current mode and level of use of some of our cherished buildings is becoming unsustainable and that may be emerging as a matter of significant priority. Perhaps if the lodge and its building were to become a centre within a community, then the maintenance of the building would likely be less of an issue as it would stand as a reflection and asset, not only of the Craft, but of the community as well.

There is a common phrase suggesting that all religions lead to God; perhaps that was something in which early speculative freemasons believed. That may explain why The Craft was condemned as being an irreligious syncretism. It cannot be denied that within the ritual there is something of the savour of salvation by works. The process is on the lines of working tools allegorically reminding us of principles contained within the volume of sacred law upon which we took our oaths and by complying with which, the outcome will be ascension to a grand lodge above. It is understandable why religious leaders are nervous about Freemasonry as it may seem to undermine their sacerdotal authority. Or, by those of a more fundamentalist position, it may be perceived to militate against salvation by faith.

Religiosity is a something that is common in humankind. It may be residual from times when revealed religion enjoyed genuine acceptation. What is felt to be religious may be understood as a desire for morality and an ethical meaningfulness of and in life. We have suggested earlier that religion may be about relationships, about warmth rather than wrath, between people and the systems with which they must interact. This brings us on to the essence of Freemasonry and what is its pride? It is of being the premier fraternity, but is it in free fall?

The primacy of fraternity:

The responses from the questionnaire provide sufficient evidence for it to be unreasonable to doubt that some of the group members really do believe and feel themselves to be in a fraternal relationship with other members; even though, they have not physically met with them. The 9/11 tragedy proved, beyond doubt to ML members that fraternity care and concern existed at a personal level between people who had never physically met. The communications that were made at the time, and in response to the tragedy, testified that our members, world wide, were united through shared feelings and experience in time, though not in space – cyber space perhaps yes. Through E-masonry people had come to "know" each other, that "each other" are part of our conscious world and that the reality of this phenomenon is perhaps a challenge to traditional Masonic thinking. This not an area for which we have proper tools of analysis – we cannot begin to understand. But, we believe it to be the case, we are a part of it and it is a part of our lives. It connects with how we live, move and have our being.

Fraternity can perhaps be understood as a bonding between people. It replicates the loyalty, support and trust that idealistically and putatively exists among flesh and blood brothers. The term "fraternity" implies a common and shared existence which effectively provides self and mutual advantage. The bonding achieves outcomes that would be greater than those that could be achieved in isolation. As such, the bonding is more important than, and over-rides, the individuality involved. In a fraternity, individuality is surrendered to the collectivity. As Freemasonry is more important than any individual Freemason, no one individual Freemason can be allowed to threaten the fraternity. On joining Freemasonry there should be a subjugation of self and a welcome embrace and belief in the benefits of an allegorical communal existence. But of course the same is true when joining any group, including perhaps, importantly, when being "received" into human society itself.

This seems to indicate that the good of all is not made up of each individual pursuing his or her own, perception of their own individual good - each person doing that which is right in their own eyes. Is this a condemnation of individualism? We definitely think not. We believe in pursuing enlightened self-interest, which by definition will not impinge on the freedom of others to pursue theirs; that is to say, a freedom that is exercised in conjunction with recognition of the rights of others to pursue theirs. Each person is entitled as much freedom that is not incompatible with the freedom of others. This is perhaps no more than a re-modelling of "Do unto others as you would have them do unto you." As such, it is not emotive, but intensely rational as it qualifies independence with a measure of interdependence – perhaps two sides of the same coin.

Shared experiences, especially those involving planning, preparation and specified outcomes do bind people together and perhaps in Freemasonry, initially at least; it is the progress to and through the chair(s) that provides the main opportunity for such bonding to occur. The attendance at less formal lodges of instruction/rehearsal and a drink afterwards, oil the wheels of this process. This may, in particular, be the case where the words of the ritual are being memorised and the director of ceremonies is able to create an expectation of high standards among both the participants (and a critique of on-lookers). Of course, this is the team model but as is common within most social groupings, people subdivide into convenient and genial cliques.

But, how significant is Masonic bonding and loyalty compared with that of family, friends, colleagues and community? We suggest that it cannot be a substitute for any of these and if that is the case, it is of low priority, not much more than the level of "fraternity" sought by say between members of a golf club or amateur theatrical society. Of course, some Freemasons do strike up serious friendships and if incorporated into wider circles these can be really profound and sustaining. But, perhaps it is the case that such friendships are rare.

We have suggested that "speculative" Freemasonry took its rise from the times when those in business and political leadership met together to discuss much more important things than Freemasonry. They were civilised people with sufficient disposable income to dine out and enjoy "good company". They were sometimes referred to as being "clubbable" people. It may well be the case that as facilities for business and political dealings became more available that meeting for more for social reasons, and conviviality, began to occur and this is perhaps when the speculative Masonic elements became more significant in terms of both time and mind. But was "speculative" Freemasonry intended to be any more than a good night out? Perhaps for some it was just a pastime, but as it gained a life of its own, for others it became more of a way of life. For these individuals, it may have provided a moral and ethical framework over and above that offered by religious organisations or required by the state; the organisation of Freemasonry providing a framework to make sense and purpose in this life recognising that both Church and state can get things both right and wrong. And, what can be wrong with such a preference, surely an excellent and worthy exercise of the freedom of choice.

But what of those for whom Freemasonry really is but a pastime and no more than a good night out, is that unworthy? Is that making a good man better? It is not for us to judge and we won't. However, we will consider the Freemasonry that we know and love and take a view on how many Freemasons we know and of whom could be persuaded that Freemasonry was for them a way of life rather than a pastime. (We have already considered those for whom Freemasonry is an add-on to their religious practice.) This we believe is a crucial question that Freemasonry and Freemasons must face and honestly consider. Indeed, even for those few Freemasons who are given to the study of nature and science, we wonder if their researches are calculated to make changes to self and the world. If not, then such studious activity – seemingly the very light of Freemasonry, could also be understood as being no more than a pastime. A commitment to study is a step of faith; what then of the self and mutual good works that may reasonably be expected to flow there from in demonstration of its vitality?

The concept of "fraternity" does imply a unity of people in a common lifestyle based on shared values. We are not aware that the members of even the most exclusive Gentlemen's clubs are referred to as being in a fraternal relationship. Perhaps the concept of fraternity in Freemasonry is, indeed, somewhat overstated – at best an ideal, worse spin and propaganda and worst of all, untrue for a significant number. However, because the bonding in Freemasonry may be of a limited nature, it does not mean that it is not worth having or is not without some significant effect. There is a milieu of care among Freemasons, celebrating and sharing each others personal joy and a commiseration in times of each others personal sorrow. We know this from our lodges and we know it from our Masonic Light E-group. But, it has to be accepted that bonding can occur between people who have never physically met. It would be unreasonable to understand this in any other way than as being masonically fraternal;

that is to say, no less fraternal in E-experience than the relationships made within and between members of lodges.

E-communication means for some, a level of quality interaction, albeit cyber, that would not be possible in the flesh and yet as least as "real" as some, or many relationships, formed around lodge meetings. E-masonry can provide a Masonic fraternity on an accessible 24/7 basis that is convenient, cost-efficient and most of all – seriously sustainable. It offers great flexibility. It can be adapted to meet the pressures of life and changing family and work circumstances. Despite being cyber, it does bond people who shared values.

Having through assiduity, study and the generation of fraternal values arrived at a situation with a level of disposable wealth, the question arises, what is to be done? The view can be taken that the goodness that emanates from Freemasonry is largely promoted, measured and understood in terms of charitable giving. If so, then E-communication can substantially simplify and make the entire process infinitely more efficient. But, is it appropriate to regard Masonic "good" as substantially expressed in terms of charitable giving?

Charitability:

The questionnaire was not calculated to enquire into any policies, procedures or practices pertaining to Masonic charitable giving and no comments of any significance were offered in response to the more open type of questions that were set. We take the view that Freemasonry has to be about so much more than charitable giving. It is a journey of discovery and awareness that through assiduity and study a person may develop and that the light of such development may inspire the lives that are touched thereby. If Freemasonry was, in practice, such an enlightened process, it would be recognised as such and would achieve positive respect from the world in general without having to leverage respectability, in particular, by charitable giving. No amount of charitable giving alone, can justify any organisation other than one specifically set up for the purpose – there are plenty of those - the Freemasonry that we have joined and support is not one of them.

There are diverse views on giving and on concepts of the "deserving poor". Speculative Freemasonry took its rise during the times prior to mass taxation. Today, and for the likely future, people are taxed on what they earn, spend and save. This is redistributed to provide protection of persons and property from attacks from without and within and also to provide forms of welfare for vulnerable people at risk of levels of poverty that would cause the poor to starve or revolt. Who in their right mind would want to join an organisation where the principle objective is to take the little that has been left after the raid by the tax gatherer? The view could be taken that the tax take is charity enough as Freemasons, of course, would never evade tax!

However, perhaps there are those who, even after legitimate contribution to the tax take, have a residual surplus and are mindful to support good and worthy causes. Given the world as it is, such people are spoiled for choice and this state of affairs is likely to remain for yet a while. There are good causes; international, national and local from which to choose. There are those in response to natural disasters, war, famine, disadvantage and misfortune. Perhaps most people have more money than what they think they have and could give more, Freemasons included.

However, there are fundamental issues to be faced when considering Freemasonry and charitable giving. That a Freemason is able to give to charity, without detriment to self or connections proves that they are successful and have passed a fundamental Masonic test of merit. If a Freemason subscribes generously to charity through Masonic routes, this will come to the attention of the leadership and may be a basis for promotion and honours and this could lead to accusations of simony.

A scope and quantum is often set for charitable appeals, "Festivals", as sometimes euphemistically described in Freemasonry. They with their attendant sub-organisations are set up to ensure that objectives and targets are achieved. It may appear to be the case that those who have provided the greatest level of support, time as well as money, will obtain Masonic recognition for so doing. This usually would take the form of Masonic promotion or honours. If such promotions are deemed to be important and considered to be worth having, this may give rise to an image of buying progress in a way which people with less time and finance would be unable to fairly compete. If the organisation is to be measured by the extensiveness of charitable giving, then it should not be surprising that those who contribute the most will obtain the greatest recognition. That is life. But, the question that remains is that of the primacy attributed to charitable giving as an appropriate priority for Freemasonry?

The case for giving to public charities, other than a vain attempt to leverage positive public recognition, has not been made. There was a time when the intrigue of "secrecy" may have made Freemasonry attractive, but during the last decades, this may no longer be the case and it is perhaps a greater likelihood that it would to be a disincentive for people to consider joining Freemasonry at all. Also, much Masonic charitable giving to public good causes was in secret and it may be felt that insufficient recognition was being achieved. Worse, organisations that were secretly in receipt of Masonic charitable giving were, in public, condemning the very existence of Freemasonry – the Anglican Church is, in public, split on receiving donations from Freemasonry.

Given that Freemasonry was suffering from negative images and that the intrigue of secrecy was giving way to a suspicion of it, Freemasonry has come out of the temple and with it, much of the secrecy that surrounds Masonic charitable giving. Yes, there have been criticisms of Freemasonry suggesting that Freemasons only look after their own. However, if this means supporting a brother or sister in times of need and/or, their dependents then fine, what is wrong with that? Indeed, if a Freemason chooses to devote all his or her charitable giving to Freemasons and/or their dependents in genuine need, who can gainsay it – we wouldn't begin to try! We take the view that giving to public good causes should be reconsidered in principle and in practice, if for no other reason than that there appears to be a growing inability for Freemasonry to support its own and to maintain its own infrastructure.

A substantial and growing number of Freemasons are over retirement age – they are also living longer. Given the general failure of both public and private institutions to provide pensions commensurate with earnings, many Freemasons in retirement are on welfare in various forms. Such levels of subsistence are not calculated to support lodge membership, jurisdiction overheads or charitable good causes. It is likely that the demographic time-bomb will generate a greater numbers of Freemasons, or their dependents, in need of increasing levels of residential and nursing care. Even with the liquidation of their assets it is likely that there will be an increasing demand for financial support. This may militate against recruitment and retention aspirations. Who would want to join an organisation largely centred on supplementing welfare provision for older people, many of whom will be, and will remain, unknown to new Freemasons?

We therefore suggest that there is a sustainability issue with Masonic charitable giving at present. Are Freemasons prepared to give in secret or is there a strategy to give openly in order to leverage respectability? We take the view that there is nothing wrong with Freemasons providing for their own in times of need and they should not be intimidated away from this by a jurisdiction with an agenda. We suggest that Freemasonry should undertake some serious strategic asset management and divest itself of property and building liabilities. That is not to say that the buildings should be torn down, but perhaps be sold to property management groups or turned over to Historical Societies or Preservation groups where perhaps the building's use could enjoy more sustainable management. We might even be able to still use the buildings!

What could be easier than online charitable giving? Nothing, but we accept that without some social pressure people,

Freemasons included, would give less. E-masonry is largely costless, charitable giving could become integral to membership. However, given that most domestic economies have contribution from both male and female, it is not for the male to decide, in isolation, the level of charitable giving that should emanate from the household. So, what might this suggest?

The mystery of gender:

It was clear from the questionnaire responses that the contribution of females was valued by a large majority and but only tolerated by a "faithful remnant" We would like to know how much, if any, is the openness of the Masonic Light E-group in terms of both cross-jurisdiction and mixed-gender, a disincentive for Freemasons who consider themselves to be "regular and recognised" to join. We cannot engage with a proposition on the lines of female masonry being "regular but not recognised". We struggle with the very concept of recognition, that is to say recognised by whom and on what basis? It seems to connote serious exclusivity but for what reason and with what authority?

We take the view that Freemasonry is too important to be confined to the male of the species and that segregation by gender is at best immaturity. Further we believe that support for male-only Freemasonry is based upon residual religiosity, the last significant cultural bastion in which a gender defined role is maintained. After all, it was Eve who first succumbed to temptation and who then seduced Adam into following suit. Yet, even within the monotheistic religions there are growing pressures for females to be allowed leadership and teaching roles. It will surely come to pass, perhaps by way of the continued decline in the numbers of male clergy and an increased role for the laity. In those polities that have signed up to universal human rights, discrimination on grounds of gender is largely unlawful in the areas of work, education and citizenship. It may not be clear if a stipendiary clergyperson is an "employee" within the meaning of the declaration of Human Rights and any local enactment.

As indicated above, Freemasons have a much reduced role and influence in local trade, education or governance. And, although Freemasonry is not just about socialising, it can be seen as such as there is the clear intention that Masonic meetings or functions would be fraternal and convivial. It must be accepted that it will be perceived as such. It is one thing for one partner in a relationship to go out and play table tennis, but, self and mutual improvement is serious whole-relationship matter. If mainstream Freemasonry is to degenerate into a dinning club, sanitised by charitable giving, then fine, it can remain male only, and remain irrelevant.

However, people who are enthused with Masonic values will not remain in such lodges or jurisdictions, but will join others with wider horizons, wherever they can be found. And found they will be via e-groups and the Internet. No longer whispered labels such as "clandestine", "irregular", "unrecognised or "unwashed" and with whom not to have contact for fear of defilement. A handful of people committed to a lifelong journey of self and mutual improvement, focussing on and from within their community, could form sustainable lodges that are integrated within the communities that they are seeking to serve and be as beacons of ethical leadership.

Perhaps mainstream jurisdictions might like to consider the possibility of posing a time frame of say ten or fifteen years by which time females would be admitted on equal terms. The option to bring this forward could be the individual decision of individual lodges. This would be a substantial signal presaging for Freemasonry in terms of its maturity, modernity and sustainability.

It may well be the case that people of the Masonic average age will have been in a relationship for some time and there is a mutual desire for space in the relationship and separate socialising. But if Freemasonry is to be attractive to younger people, who have been in relationships for less time, separate socialising may not be attractive, even a significant detriment for those considering membership. There may be a preference for socialising, for one or both in a relationship, in an environment that is single gender. On the other hand, a mixed gender environment may be perceived as a threat to relationships. But, such an environment is a norm in work, education and citizenship; indeed, across all significant cultural undertakings. There may well be something inadequate, immature and un-enlightened about apprehension to mixed gender Freemasonry; but of course it does exist and is growing.

Again, although we accept that there may be good reasons for space in a relationship and single gender socialising, we confirm our view that the teachings of Freemasonry are too important to provide such a facility. If separate gender socialising is desired then fine, but let this be undertaken in activities of lesser importance. Freemasonry is, through individual enlightenment, for the development and fulfilment of humankind. Perhaps it is the case that the gender issue is providing mainstream Freemasonry with both a wake-up call and a grow-up call. Perhaps it is really is the case that to ignore the signs of the times is to invite extinction, a process that may well insidiously and inexorably be in effect. In this work we have sought to share our experience as E-masons and we are hoping that there may be some ideas that will help to assist the arrest of the onward march of decline and an adaptation to meet the demands of the future.

Where might the journey lead?

In an organisation celebrating traditional values in a traditional way, it is inevitable that the accommodations of either frequent or rapid changes are not in its nature. But does not nature itself teach us that time and tide wait for no man, not even Masonic-man. With the strength and decisiveness of a natural phenomenon in full force, E-communication has tossed aside most in its path and altered the topography of the land. It has changed horizons in terms of what is global and what is local and this revised juxtaposition has yet to be fully recognised, assimilated or disseminated. What is to be decided on a global basis and what may be decided locally? Clarity is needed on how engagement by individuals is possible in global matters and what, without let or hindrance, can be decided at the street corner? What levels are there, if any, between the global stratosphere and the street corner, how might they be recognised and legitimised? What scope is there for alternatives to top-down dictatorship?

Yes, we do seek a Freemasonry that is both truly and universally inclusive yet powerfully effective locally. This may mean the removal of a number of interim layers, far fewer in rank and more in the ranks. It may mean a more local focus; it may entail treating religious systems as being alternatives to Freemasonry and a distinct demarcation and operational disengagement there from. It may require a substantial rationalisation of resources, their scope and target, and will require recognising females on equal human terms.

Whilst then we have run with the values of work and education, we have sought to enhance the value of participatory citizenship, sought a clean break with the appearances of religion, extended fraternity, qualified charity and advocated co-masonry. Where might all this leave the ritual? It would seem that there are fewer and fewer learning it by heart. We would claim that given the nature of the subject matter there will be less and less engagement with it on the part of younger adults. We take the view, albeit sadly, that the ritual does not provide moral instruction in anything like a day by day ethical reality. The periodic changes that are made to ritual books are met with cynicism and resistance and there is little consistency of practice even within jurisdictions, each doing that which is right in their own eyes.

The answer is increased commitment by Freemasons to education in all the forms that are now possible, especially through E-distance learning. Education could gradually replace or reduce ritual. Yes, back to the process of enlightenment and as practiced in the early days of "speculative" Freemasonry with up to date leading-edge lectures and demonstrations in the lodge. And, in line with the thrust of what we have suggested earlier, Freemasons could be a key provider of any education in the wider locality and community.

This is a time for "heads up" by Freemasons to seize the unprecedented opportunities of the future. There is a human vacuum at the heart of many communities and a yearning for the right people to come in to fill and to fulfil. Freemasons with the E of futurity are surely those people.

Table 1

Age Group	Respondents	Percentage
20-29	6	5.3
30-39	26	23.3
40-49	25	22.3
50-59	32	28.6
60-69	17	15.1
70-79	6	5.3

Table 2

Jurisdiction	% of Masonic Light	% of responses
American Federation Human Rights	1.36	2.56
GL Canada/Ontario	2.32	5.98
Le Droit Humain	2.59	4.27
UGLE	6.68	9.4
GL Virginia	1.36	4.27

Table 3 – Years in Freemasonry

Years of Masonic Service	Respondents	Percentage
1-10	60	55.5
11-20	18	16.5
21+	30	28

Table 4 – Years in E-Masonry

Years of E-Masonry	Respondents	Percentage
1	22	20
2	12	11
3	14	13
4	12	11
5	16	15
6	10	9
7	5	6
8+	17	15

Table 5 – E-Masonry Groups Joined

E-Masonry Groups Joined	Respondents	Percentage
1-3	57	53
4-6	31	29.5
7-10	12	11.5
11-19	3	3
20-40	4	4

Table 6

Masonic Service Years	E-Masonry Years	Number of Masonic E-Groups Joined
1	1	4-6
1	1	1-3
1	1	1-3
1	1	1-3
1	1	1-3
1	1	7-10
2	2	1-3
2	1	1-3
2	1	1-3
2	2	1-3
2	2	11-15
3	1	1-3
3	1	1-3
3	2	1-3
3	2	4-6
3	3	7-10
3	3	4-6
3	1	1-3
4	1	1-3
4	1	1-3
4	4	4-6
4	3	4-6
4	4	4-6
4	4	7-10
4	2	1-3
4	1	1-3
5	5	11-15
5	3	1-3
5	2	4-6
5	3	7-10

Table 6 (cont.)

Masonic Service Years	E-Masonry Years	Number of Masonic E-Groups Joined
5	1	1-3
5	4	1-3
5	5	4-6
5	5	4-6
6	3	1-3
6	4	1-3
6	3	4-6
6	5	1-3
6	1	1-3
6	3	1-3
7	1	1-3
7	5	4-6
8	2	1-3
8	5	11-15
8	2	4-6
8	6	4-6
8	8	4-6
8	8	11-15
8	8	1-3
9	5	1-3
9	2	1-3
9	9	4-6
9	7	1-3
9	8	11-15
10	10	1-3
10	8	1-3
10	10	1-3
10	9	16-40
10	7	1-3

Table 7
Respondents with no negative sides of E-Masonry

Age	Avg. 30	33	36	42	44	47	49	52	52	57	59
Masonic years	2	8	1	8	2	10	12	22	4	3	
E-Masonry years	2	8	1	5	1	10	5	-	4		

69		70	74	51	
24		32	15	38	13
3		-	8	-	4	4.6

More Masonic Books from Cornerstone

The Three Distinct Knocks
by Samuel Pritchard
6x9 Softcover 100 pages
ISBN 1613421826

Origin of the Royal Arch
by George Oliver
Softcover 202 pages
ISBN 1613420730

In His Own (w)Rite
by Michael R. Poll
6x9 Softcover 176 pages
Retail Price: $15.95
ISBN: 1-61342-017-X

Outline of the Rise and Progress of Freemasonry in Louisiana
by James B. Scot
Introduction by Alain Bernheim
Afterword by Michael R. Poll
8x10 Softcover 180 pages
ISBN 1-934935-31-X

Military Lodges: The Apron and the Sword
by Robert Freke Gould
6x9 Softcover 252 pages
ISBN 161342177X

The Master Workman or True Masonic Guide
by Henry C. Atwood
6x9 Softcover 396 pages
ISBN 1613420528

Cornerstone Book Publishers
www.cornerstonepublishers.com

More Masonic Books from Cornerstone

Masonic Enlightenment
The Philosophy, History and Wisdom of Freemasonry
Edited by Michael R. Poll
6 x 9 Softcover 180 pages
ISBN 1-887560-75-0

Morgan: The Scandal That Shook Freemasonry
by Stephen Dafoe
Foreword by Arturo de Hoyos
6x9 Softcover 484 pages
ISBN 1-934935-54-9

Masonic Questions and Answers
by Paul M. Bessel
6 x 9 Softcover 144 pages
ISBN 1-887560-59-9

Our Stations and Places - Masonic Officer's Handbook
by Henry G. Meacham
Revised by Michael R. Poll
6 x 9 Softcover 164 pages
ISBN: 1-887560-63-7

Knights & Freemasons: The Birth of Modern Freemasonry
By Albert Pike & Albert Mackey
Edited by Michael R. Poll
Foreword by S. Brent Morris
6 x 9 Softcover 178 pages
ISBN 1-887560-66-1

Robert's Rules of Order: Masonic Edition
Revised by Michael R. Poll
6 x 9 Softcover 212 pages
ISBN 1-887560-07-6

Cornerstone Book Publishers
www.cornerstonepublishers.com

More Masonic Books from Cornerstone

The Freemasons Key
A Study of Masonic Symbolism
Edited by Michael R. Poll
6 x 9 Softcover 244 pages
ISBN: 1-887560-97-1

The Ancient and Accepted Scottish Rite
in Thirty-Three Degrees
by Robert B. Folger
Introduction by Michael R. Poll
ISBN: 1-934935-88-3

The Bonseigneur Rituals
Edited by Gerry L. Prinsen
Foreword by Michael R. Poll
8x10 Softcover 2 volumes 574 pages
ISBN 1-934935-34-4

A.E. Waite: Words From a Masonic Mystic
Edited by Michael R. Poll
Foreword by Joseph Fort Newton
6 x 9 Softcover 168 pages
ISBN: 1-887560-73-4

Freemasons and Rosicrucians - the Enlightened
by Manly P. Hall
Edited by Michael R. Poll
6 x 9 Softcover 152 pages
ISBN: 1-887560-58-0

Masonic Words and Phrases
Edited by Michael R. Poll
6 x 9 Softcover 116 pages
ISBN: 1-887560-11-4

Cornerstone Book Publishers
www.cornerstonepublishers.com

More Masonic Books from Cornerstone

Historical Inquiry into the Origins of the Ancient and Accepted Scottish Rite
by James Foulhouze
Foreword by Michael R. Poll
6x9 Softcover 216 pages
ISBN 1-613420-26-9

A General History of Freemasonry
by Emmanuel Rebold
Translated by J. Fletcher Brennan
Softcover 434 pages
ISBN 1-934935-81-6

Lectures of the Ancient and Primitive Rite of Freemasonry
by John Yarker
6x9 Softcover 218 pages
ISBN 1-934935-10-7

The Schism Between the Scotch & York Rites
by Charles Laffon de Ladébat
6x9 Softcover 66 pages
ISBN 1-934935-33-6

The Ceremony of Initiation
by W.L. Wilmshurst
6x9 Softcover 74 pages
ISBN 1-934935-02-6

Museum and Memorial: Ten Years of Masonic Writings
by Mark A. Tabbert
6 x 9 Softcover 176 pages
ISBN 1-934935-83-2

Cornerstone Book Publishers
www.cornerstonepublishers.com

www.ingramcontent.com/pod-product-compliance
Lightning Source LLC
Chambersburg PA
CBHW031207270326
41931CB00006B/443